CW00495798

OSPREY AIRCRAFT OF THE ACE

Spitfire Mk I/II Aces 1939-41

B
553

SERIES EDITOR: TONY HOLMES

OSPREY AIRCRAFT OF THE ACES • 12

Spitfire Mk I/II Aces 1939-41

Dr Alfred Price

OSPREY AEROSPACE

First published in Great Britain in 1996
by Osprey, an imprint of Reed Consumer Books Limited
Michelin House, 81 Fulham Road, London SW3 6RB
and Auckland, Melbourne, Singapore and Toronto

ISBN 1 85532627 2

Edited by Tony Holmes
Page design by TT Designs, T & S Truscott
Profile Commentary by Tony Holmes and Dr Alfred Price
Chapter Seven written by Tony Holmes
Captions by Tony Holmes and Dr Alfred Price

Cover Artwork by Iain Wyllie
Aircraft Profiles by Keith Fretwell and Mark Rolfe
Figure Artwork by Mike Chappell
Scale Drawings by Mark Styling

Printed in Hong Kong

The editor would like to thank Wg Cdr George Unwin and Grp Capt Desmond Sheen for agreeing to be interviewed for this volume, and *Aeroplane Monthly*, Aerospace Publishing, RAF Hendon Museum, Norman Franks, Don Healey, Dr Jan P Koniarek, Frank Mason, Bruce Robertson and Jerry Scutts for providing additional photographs.

EDITOR'S NOTE

To make this new series as authoritative as possible, the editor would be extremely interested in hearing from any individual who may have relevant photographs, documentation or first-hand experiences relating to the elite pilots, and their aircraft, of the various theatres of war. Any material used will be fully credited to its original source. Please write to Tony Holmes at 1 Bradbourne Road, Sevenoaks, Kent, TN13 3PZ, Great Britain.

Front cover

On 15 September 1940 (now celebrated as Battle of Britain Day) the *Jagdwaffe* lost over 20 Bf 109Es in combat across southern England, three of which fell to the guns of No 19 Sqn's leading ace, Flt Sgt George Unwin. Of this trio of kills, one was claimed during a morning patrol over south London and the remaining pair near Lydd, on the Kent coast, during a mid-afternoon 'Big Wing' sortie. This specially commissioned artwork by Iain Wyllie shows Unwin having just downed his second *Emil* (Bf 109E-4 Werk-Nr 3759, flown by Stab I./JG 77's Oblt Herbert Kunze, who was *Gruppe* Adjutant), and now firing on his third kill. Having set a course for the Pas de Calais following the completion of their escort mission to London, the two *Jagdflieger* had been spotted by Unwin at distance and chased for some considerable period of time before the latter got into a position to attack at an altitude approaching 25,000 ft – neither German saw their lone attacker.

The Spitfire Mk IA used by the No 19 Sqn pilot (X4179) was a near-factory fresh machine which had served briefly with No 266 Sqn. After a glorious fortnight with Flt Sgt Unwin, during which time he used it to score four kills over Bf 109Es, X4179 was passed to No 609 Sqn, with whom it served until early 1941. The Spitfire's frontline career continued with Nos 66, 131 and 140 Sqns during that year, before it was relegated to OTU service. The fighter was finally written off when it overturned following a wheels up landing on 24 October 1943 at Eshott whilst assigned to No 57 OTU

CONTENTS

AUTHOR'S INTRODUCTION

Without doubt the Spitfire was the most famous fighter type ever to serve in the Royal Air Force, and the most famous action in which it took part was the Battle of Britain. This book describes the operational career of the Mark I and Mark II versions of the fighter in the period before, during and immediately after that epic action. Virtually from the moment it entered service, the Spitfire underwent a continual programme of modification as Supermarine engineers worked to improve the airframe and Rolls-Royce produced new and more powerful versions of the Merlin engine.

Of course, the Spitfire would have amounted to nothing without the skills of the pilots who flew it. This book also describes many of those who took it into action and, after receiving credit for five or more aerial victories, gained the status of ace. In listing the pilots' credited victory scores, I have considered only the confirmed victory claims – unconfirmed claims have been omitted.

Several good friends contributed material and photographs to assist with the preparation of this book. In particular I am grateful to Norman Franks, Dilip Sarkar and Bruce Robertson. Ted Hooton gave me the benefit of his vast research into Spitfire modification states, as well as assisting the artists so that they could produce the most accurate colour plates of the aces' aircraft ever published. Yet again I offer my profound thanks to Chris Shores and Clive Williams for allowing me to use material from their superb reference book *Aces High*. For anyone wishing to learn more about the careers of the RAF fighter aces, this book is strongly recommended.

Alfred Price
January 1996

INITIAL ENCOUNTERS

This evocative line-up shot of Spitfires from the initial production batch was taken by the legendary Charles E Brown during the first No 19 Sqn Spitfire Press Day, held at Duxford on 4 May 1939. The aircraft are seen being readied by their groundcrews for the squadron 'Battle Formation' flypast, which signalled the end of the day's activities at the Cambridgeshire fighter station. All 11 Spitfires are fitted with the original two-bladed wooden propellers, narrow aerial masts, unprotected windscreens and ring-and-bead gun sights. The second and fifth aircraft in the line also still boast the initial, flat-topped, canopy, while most of the others have the later bulged-top type. Note also that the closest aircraft is the only Spitfire to lack an individual letter code (*Vickers*)

Spitfires first fired their guns in anger on 6 September 1939, three days after Great Britain declared war on Germany. At 06.45 hours, the early warning radar station at Canewdon in Essex reported a force of unidentified aircraft coming in from the east. During the minutes that followed, the strength of the incoming force increased to five formations each estimated at between six and twelve aircraft. In fact, due to a failure of the radar's sensing system, aircraft flying to the *west* of the station appeared on the radar screen as if they were to the *east* of it (i.e. in the direction from which a German attack was expected). Several fighter units scrambled to intercept the 'intruders' and headed towards the Thames Estuary. As they did so, their radar echoes joined with those from the phantom raiding force seemingly approaching from the east. The result was a chain reaction, the 'hostile force' appearing to grow larger each time an RAF squadron took off. Within a few minutes the number of 'incoming' formations had increased to 12, all now designated as 'hostile'. It looked as if the Luftwaffe was about to launch its predicted aerial onslaught against London. Across eastern England the air defence system came to full alert and at 06:55 hours the air raid sirens sounded in the capital.

The weather over the Thames Estuary that morning was poor, with banks of thick cloud over south-east England. Anti-aircraft batteries at

Thameshaven and Sheerness engaged the 'enemy aircraft' as they came within range and shot down a Blenheim fighter and damaged a Spitfire of No 65 Sqn. A few minutes later, near Colchester, the leader of a section of Spitfires from No 74 Sqn saw a formation of 'enemy aircraft' some distance ahead of him. With the sun glinting off the aircraft it was difficult to identify their type, but from the radio calls it seemed clear there were enemy machines nearby. The three Spitfires dived on the two machines at the rear of the formation and shot down each with an accurate burst. However, these 'enemy planes' turned out to be Hurricanes from No 56 Sqn. The latter broke formation to avoid further attacks, as their leader repeatedly called on the radio to his pilots 'Do not retaliate. They are friendly!' Although the situation quickly resolved itself, at the end of it both sides nervously eyed each other.

At 08:00 hours the so-called 'Battle of Barking Creek' reached its inglorious conclusion, as fighters ran short of fuel and began returning to base. Only then was it clear that no German planes had been in the area that morning. For Air Chief Marshal (ACM) Dowding, the Commander in Chief (C-in-C) of Fighter Command, the incident was a bitter blow. What had caused his carefully devised system of fighter control to enter a self-destruct mode? An inquiry determined that the root cause of the incident was the technical fault at the radar station at Canewdon. Once the presence of the 'enemy planes' had been established, the clash that followed was almost inevitable given that the defenders were inexperienced in war, and over-quick on the trigger. The incident highlighted the need for a means of distinguishing friendly aircraft on radar. Such a device, the IFF (Identification Friend or Foe) equipment, was already in production, but now its introduction received a higher priority than previously. The station commander at North Weald and the two Spitfire pilots who shot down Hurricanes later stood trial by court martial, the former receiving a cursory punishment and the latter being exonerated.

Six of the original pilots to fly Spitfires with No 19 Sqn – Flg Offs Pace, Robinson, Clouston, Banham, Ball and, in the chair, Thomas. Two achieved ace status in 1940, Wilfred Clouston being credited with 9 aircraft destroyed, 3 shared destroyed, 1 and 1 shared probably destroyed and 1 shared damaged, and George Ball claiming 6 aircraft destroyed, 1 shared destroyed and 3 damaged (*No 19 Sqn Archive*)

The first Spitfire write-off. On 16 August 1938 Plt Off Gordon Sinclair of No 19 Sqn touched down at Duxford at the end of his first flight in the Spitfire, only to have the port wheel break away and the aircraft flip on to its back. He emerged from the incident without injury to himself or to his reputation, for the cause of the accident was traced to faulty metal in the axle stub. Sinclair scored six kills with No 19 Sqn over Dunkirk in May/June 1940, and became one of the first Spitfire aces. During the Battle of Britain he flew Hurricanes with No 310 'Czech' Sqn, increasing his score to 10 destroyed and 1 damaged (*No 19 Sqn Archive*)

Spitfire final assembly at Eastleigh on 23 January 1939. In front of the aircraft nearest to the camera is the upper fuel tank, which is about to be fitted forward of the cockpit. Part of the first batch of 310 (308 delivered) Spitfires ordered by the Ministry of Supply on 3 June 1936, the airframes seen in this view were primarily issued to Nos 54 and 74 Sqns in the final weeks of February 1939 (*via Aeroplane*)

Deployment for War

By the start of World War 2 the Supermarine works at Southampton had delivered 306 Spitfires to the RAF. Of this total, 187 were currently serving with 11 Fighter Command Squadrons (Nos 19, 41, 54, 65, 66, 72, 74, 602, 603, 609 and 611), and a further 71 were held at maintenance units, ready to be despatched to the frontline to replace losses. Eleven Spitfires were serving as trials machines, either with the makers or with the various service test establishments, one was allocated to the Central Flying School for use by those writing the Pilot's Notes on the aircraft, and the remaining 36 airframes had been struck off charge, mostly due to flying accidents.

Spitfire Is of No 65 Sqn pictured shortly before the outbreak of war. The aircraft nearest the camera, K9906/FZ-L, was picked up from the Supermarine factory by the squadron following its pre-delivery flight checks and flown back to their Hornchurch base on 24 March 1939. It was then allocated to Flg Off Robert Stanford Tuck, who would later become one of the first Spitfire pilots to be credited with five victories. K9906 was transferred to No 64 Sqn in April 1940, and flew throughout the Battle of Britain with this unit (*Vickers*)

Plt Off Paul Webb of No 602 'City of Glasgow' Sqn pictured in his Spitfire early in the war when the aircraft bore the initial ZT code letters. Webb was one of the pilots who took part in the initial engagement of enemy aircraft by Spitfires on 16 October 1939 when a Ju 88A-1 of Stab I./KG 30 was downed over the Firth of Forth. By the end of the Battle of Britain he was credited with 3 destroyed, 3 shared destroyed and 5 damaged, although he had missed the final six weeks of the campaign after suffering a broken wrist on 9 September during a forced landing in the badly shot up K9910 (*Cameron*)

During the early months of the war all Spitfire fighter units were based in Great Britain. Thus, during the so-called 'Phoney War' period which lasted until May 1940, these fighters encountered enemy aircraft only on the rare occasions when the latter ventured close to the British Isles. The Spitfire first went into action against genuinely hostile aircraft on 16 October 1939. On that day nine Junkers Ju 88A-1s of 1./KG 30 delivered an attack on Royal Navy warships in the Firth of Forth, and Nos 602 and 603 Sqns, based at Drem and Turnhouse respectively, were scrambled to engage the raiders. Flt Lt Pat Gifford of No 603 Sqn shot down one bomber and Flt Lts George Pinkerton and Archie McKellar (who would later score 17 kills on Hurricane Is, including five in one day, with No 605 Sqn during 1940) of No 602 Sqn destroyed another. Fighters of No 603 Sqn engaged yet another Ju 88 and shot out one of its engines, but it managed to escape back to Germany.

In the months that followed Spitfires had occasional encounters with individual German bombers, minelayers or reconnaissance aircraft. For the most part, however, this was a period of expansion of the force and of intensive training for the battles to come. By the beginning of May 1940 a further eight squadrons (Nos 64, 92, 152, 222, 234, 266, 610 and 616) had received Spitfires, thus bringing the strength of the force up to nineteen squadrons.

The 'Phoney War' came to an abrupt end on 10 May 1940 when German forces launched their all-out offensive in the west. The initial air actions in that uneven contest took place well beyond the range of the Spitfire units based in southern England, but that situation was soon to change – on 12 May, two days into the campaign, Spitfires of No 66 Sqn flew a brief patrol over The Hague, and in a short skirmish with the Luftwaffe, they claimed the destruction of one enemy aircraft. On the following day the same unit was in action again, this time over Rotterdam, and made further victory claims, but also lost one of its own in return.

In a long war of attrition, an efficient organisation for the repair of aircraft is essential. This Spitfire had been damaged in a landing accident in late 1939, and is seen disassembled prior to being repaired at the Morris Motors factory at Oxford. Following its restoration to airworthiness, the fighter flew with No 266 Sqn during the Battle of Britain (*via Robertson*)

It appears that the first dogfight between Messerschmitt Bf 109s and Spitfires (from No 74 Sqn) took place near Calais on 23 May, without loss on either side. In the days that followed the action escalated, and many more Spitfire units entered the battle. For the first time the RAF's fastest fighter was in action against enemy machines of equivalent performance – now the Spitfire had to show that it could take punishment as well as dish it out.

On 25 May the first Allied troops were evacuated from the port of Dunkirk. Also on that day No 54 Sqn escorted a squadron of Fleet Air Arm Swordfish delivering an attack on German troops between Gravelines and Calais. The biplanes completed their attack without interference, and headed for home. Once they were safely on their way the Spitfires were free to head south looking for trouble. They soon found it, as Plt Off Colin Gray later recalled;

'Suddenly, we found ourselves in amongst a gaggle of 109s. I opened fire at one of them, but stopped when I noticed smoke coming back over my wings. That shook me – I thought somebody was firing at me. I pulled round hard but there was nobody there – what I had seen was cordite smoke blowing back from my own guns. I looked back at the Messerschmitt and saw Sgt John Norwell (who would later become an ace, Ed.) on its tail and the German pilot baling out.'

Norwell and Gray would each be credited with half shares in the destruction of the Messerschmitt. As the German fighter went down, Gray spent too long watching his victim – an error that nearly cost him his life.

'Suddenly, there was one Hell of a row, like somebody running a bar along a piece of corrugated iron. The stick was knocked out of my hand and ended up in the left-hand corner of the cockpit, and my aircraft flicked into a spiral dive. I grabbed the stick and hauled back on it, and the Spitfire responded immediately and started to climb. I looked behind but didn't see anyone – the German pilot had not repeated my mistake of following me down. I selected +12 lbs (emer-

Spitfires of No 66 Sqn drawn together for rapid refuelling at Duxford in early 1940. Once the Fighter Command airfields came under threat of attack, aircraft were dispersed and refuelled individually so as not to offer such an inviting target

Spitfires of No 611 'West Lancashire' Sqn seen at Digby in February 1940 during a Fighter Command Press Day – note all the civilian reporters/photographers in Trilby hats and overcoats behind the Mark I in the foreground, and the three-aircraft section 'scrambled' to 'beat up' the Lincolnshire fighter station. The small trolleys beside the aircraft were accumulator trolleys used for engine starting (*via Scutts*)

gency boost) and continued my climb – the airspeed indicator read 240 mph, and I thought "This is bloody marvellous!" (the normal speed for a Spitfire in a steep climb was about 190 mph indicated). But then, as I continued the climb, the Spitfire began to shudder and it seemed as if it was going to stall. I couldn't understand it – the airspeed indicated still read 240 mph. I eased the stick forwards, but still it read 240 mph . . . Then I realised what had happened – my pitot head had been shot away, and the needle had dropped to the 240 mph position on the dial under gravity. . .

'I levelled out and took stock of the situation. One cannon shell had gone through the port aileron, and that was what had knocked the stick out of my hand and sent the aircraft into the violent spiral dive which shook off the Messerschmitt. The airspeed indicator was out, and there was no air pressure or hydraulic pressure. That meant that I had no flaps or brakes and I couldn't lower the undercarriage using the main hydraulic system. As I approached Hornchurch I blew down the undercarriage using the emergency carbon dioxide system, and saw the "undercarriage down" sticks push up through the wings and two green lights come on to indicate that the wheels were down and locked.

The national press were frequent visitors to fighter stations across the UK during the first months of war, this shot of a mock scramble (which again features No 611 Sqn) being taken during *Flight*'s tour of RAF Drem, near Edinburgh, on 8 April 1940 – the last day of the 'Phoney War'. This brace of 'West Lancashire' Spitfires happened to be in the right place at the right time when it came to being included in the photos taken on this date, as the unit was still very much Digby-based in the spring of 1940 (*via Aeroplane*)

Groundcrewmen working on Spitfire K9962 of No 602 Sqn at Drem in early March 1940. This aircraft wears the red lion and the Cross of St Andrew flag (as depicted on the unit's official crest) over a Swastika beneath its cockpit. Two kill markings in the unique style of crossed out Swastika flags (complete with flagpoles) denote the Spitfire's effective employment during the early skirmishes over the Forth of Firth in the autumn/winter of 1939/40. Its pilot, Sqn Ldr A D Farquhar, was credited with shared kills over two He 111s and a Ju 88 between 16 October 1939 and 22 February 1940, plus a shared damaged against another Heinkel bomber. No 602 Sqn's first wartime OC, he was promoted to Wing Commander and posted to command RAF Martlesham Heath soon after this photo was taken. K9962 was later issued to No 222 Sqn on 3 September 1940, but was shot down within 24 hours by Bf 109s over Kent, its pilot, Sgt J W Ramshaw, being killed (*via Aeroplane*)

'The landing was very difficult. With the flaps up one came in at a different attitude than usual and, of course, I had no idea of my airspeed – the indicator still read 240 mph! The first time, I came in too fast. The station commander at Hornchurch, Wg Cdr "Daddy" Bouchier, was watching my performance and was overheard to say "The silly young bugger. He's going too fast. He'll never get in!" He was right. I got my wheels almost on the ground, realised I was not going to make it and took off again. The second time I stood well back from the airfield, and dragged the aircraft in at just above stalling speed. That time I landed, and as I touched down the elevator cable finally parted and the control column collapsed back into my stomach.

'On examination of the Spitfire afterwards it was found that a cannon shell had gone through the inspection hatch in the rear fuselage and exploded inside. Splinters from the shell had slashed their way out of the skinning, leaving it looking like a cheese grater. The air bottles had been knocked out, so were the batteries. There were bullet holes up and down the fuselage and, of course, the cannon shell through the aileron. From the entry and exit holes of the bullets it was clear the Messerschmitt had dived on me from the right and above – it had been a very neat piece of deflection shooting.'

'The Spitfire (N3173) was put up on trestles and people from Vickers were invited to come and look at it to see how much it had suffered. It was the first Hornchurch aircraft that had been fairly well clobbered and still got back. Soon there would be many others.'

Colin Gray would become one of the most successful Spitfire pilots, and also the top-scoring New Zealander of the war. Yet of his many actions, his most memorable was the one when lack of experience so nearly brought a premature end to his flying career.

Flt Lt Wilfred Clouston of No 19 Sqn pictured beside K9854 following a forced landing on Newmarket racecourse after his No 2 ran into his tail during a formation training exercise on 6 October 1939. The latter's propeller had chewed away about half of the rudder and elevators. This machine had originally been issued to No 66 Sqn, who shared Duxford with No 19 Sqn, on the last day of 1938. K9854 then spent two months at Farnborough on trials work in the spring, before being sent back to Duxford for service with No 19 Sqn in May 1939 (*No 19 Sqn Archive*)

The operations to cover the Dunkirk evacuation in May and early June 1940 saw the first large scale commitment of Spitfires into action. During the attendant actions the new fighter showed that it could take punishment as well as dish it out. This aircraft, flown by Plt Off Oswald Pigg of No 72 Sqn, was badly shot up by a Ju 87 over Dunkirk on 2 June – the RAF pilot had earlier downed a Stuka prior to being shot up attacking a second dive-bomber. Although Pigg had no flaps, brakes or aileron control, he succeeded in getting both the aircraft back across the Channel and executing a copybook belly landing at his unit's Gravesend base.

Sgt Pigg was later shot down and killed in P9458 after being jumped by Bf 109s during a late morning patrol by No 72 Sqn on 1 September 1940 over Kent – profiled ace Des Sheen (see Chapter Seven) was also shot down in this action

As the air fighting escalated both sides suffered losses. The evacuation ended during the early morning darkness on 3 June 1940. By then three Spitfire pilots, Flt Lts Alan Deere and Robert Stanford Tuck, from Nos 54 and 92 Sqns respectively, and Flg Off Gordon Sinclair of No 19 Sqn, had each been credited with five or more victories. Fighter Command had, however, suffered heavily in covering the evacuation, losing 72 Spitfires – nearly one–third of its frontline strength of these aircraft. It was as well the operation ended when it did, for Sir Hugh Dowding had no choice but to accept this punishing loss rate so long as it continued. There could be no thought of abandoning the Royal Navy and the Allied troops to the mercies of the Luftwaffe.

Night Interlude

The Air Ministry specification for the Spitfire called for a 'day and night fighter', and night air defence was part of its operational role throughout the first year of the war. Indeed, when the Spitfire first saw action as a night fighter it seemed that it was highly effective in this role.

The first large scale attack by the Luftwaffe on inland targets in Great Britain took place on the night of 18-19 June 1940. Some 70 bombers from KG 4 set out to attack the airfields at Leconfield and Mildenhall, oil storage tanks on Canvey Island and a range of other targets.

The raiders, believing they had little to fear from night fighters, crossed the coast at altitudes between 10,000 and 15,000 ft and headed for their targets. It was a brilliant moonlight night with clear skies, however, and the bomber crews had to pay for their error. Blenheim fighters and Hurricanes took off to engage the intruders, as did the Spitfires of Nos 19 and 74 Sqns. Flt Lt 'Sailor' Malan of No 74 Sqn caught sight of a He 111P of 4./KG 4 near Felixstowe and promptly shot it down. The Spitfire pilot resumed his patrol and a few minutes later he observed more searchlight activity near Southend. He climbed to 12,000 ft and headed into the area, and soon afterwards a clutch of searchlights held another Heinkel in their beams. Malan closed in to attack it and afterwards he reported; 'I gave it two five-second bursts

During the operations to cover the Dunkirk evacuation Fighter Command lost 72 Spitfires. This anonymous aircraft, being picked over by German souvenir hunters, had made a crash landing on one of the beaches near Dunkirk (*via Willis*)

This Mark I, flown by Plt Off Alistair Grant of No 602 Sqn, is pictured in its revetment at Drem in April 1940. The eight guns, and associated ammunition bays, of the Spitfire Mk I/IA's 'A' wing were covered by 22 panels secured by 150 turn buttons. It was estimated that a proficient four-man re-arming team could turn a Spitfire around in 30 minutes. The diamond-shaped marking on the wing was gas-sensitive paint applied in order to detect poison gas (*via Cameron*)

and observed bullets entering all over the enemy aircraft, with slight deflection as he was turning to port. Enemy aircraft emitted heavy smoke and I observed one parachute open very close . . .' Malan followed the falling aircraft (of Stab./ KG 4) and saw it crash into the ground near Chelmsford.

Spitfires of No 19 Sqn were also active, having been vectored to engage enemy aircraft reported near Newmarket. Flg Off John Petre sighted a Heinkel (again of 4./KG 4) and was closing in to engage when suddenly he had to pull away to avoid a Blenheim fighter after the same bomber. Petre realigned himself on the intruder and opened fire. He saw his tracer rounds strike one of the engines, which immediately caught fire. At that moment, however, his own aircraft was lit up by a searchlight. That allowed the German rear gunner to get in an accurate burst, which set fire to the Spitfire's fuel tank. Petre bailed out of the blazing fighter and reached the ground with severe burns to his face and hands. Soon afterwards the Blenheim and the Heinkel both went down out of control and crashed.

Flg Off George Ball, also from No 19 Sqn, sighted another Heinkel (of 6./KG 4) illuminated by searchlights near Southend. It took him five minutes to get into a firing position, but his accurate bursts scored hits on both engines and the Heinkel crashed on land near the Thames Estuary. This was Ball's last Spitfire kill, although he went on to claim another four more victories and one shared flying Hurricanes with No 242 Sqn later that summer.

Elsewhere that night Blenheim fighters shot down a further Heinkel, and damaged yet another so seriously that it was wrecked during the crash landing near

Calais. Altogether, the action cost KG 4 six He 111s destroyed (all confirmed in German records), four of them to Spitfires. Exactly a week later on the night of 26th-27th, Spitfires fought another successful action. A He 111P-2 of 3./KG 4 fell to the guns of Plt Offs R Smith and R Marples (the latter going on to achieve ace status with No 41 Sqn) of No 616 Sqn, whilst Flt Lt H MacDonald (5 kills, 3 shared and 2 probables) of No 603 Sqn got a He 111H-3 of 3./KG 26 – a second machine from this unit fell to Flg Off A Johnstone (his first of an eventual total of 7 and 1 shared destroyed and 1 probable) of No 602 Sqn and Flg Off J Haig of No 603 Sqn, possibly with some help from AA gunners.

The Luftwaffe soon learned its lesson from those early night attacks on Britain, however. German aircraft operating over the British Isles at night then flew at altitudes between 18,000 and 20,000 ft, where they were almost beyond the reach of the low-powered searchlights. There the raiders could operate with near impunity, although their crews found it more difficult to find the targets, and as a result their bombing was far less accurate.

In the weeks to follow Spitfires flew numerous night interception sorties, but never again would they achieve successes to compare with those in the latter half of June. More often, the pilots flying night interception patrols in Spitfires had to fight against the elements, and sometimes the latter won. Flg Off Trevor 'Wimpy' Wade (who later became an ace with 6 and 4 shared destroyed and 6 probables) of No 92 Sqn wrote an account of his patrol on the night of 27/28 July which perfectly illustrates the problems encountered;

In the first six months of the war, the Auxiliary squadrons in Scotland saw more action than any other units in Fighter Command, either in the UK or abroad in France. One of those squadrons was No 602, based at Drem and led by former Glasgow stockbroker Sqn Ldr Andrew Farquhar – indeed, so successful was his unit that he was awarded one of the first DFCs of the war on 1 March 1940. The other pilots that made 'ace' in this official group shot – taken in early 1940 – were Flg Off P C Webb (3 and 3 shared destroyed and 5 damaged), Flg Off A A McKellar (17 and 3 shared destroyed, 5 probables and 3 damaged – only 2 shared on Spitfires though), Flt Lt A V R Johnstone (7 and 2 shared, 1 probable, 6 and 1 damaged) and Flt Lt R F Boyd (14 and 7 shared destroyed, 3 probables and 7 damaged)

'Soon after getting settled down on the patrol line over the Swansea area – marked, incidentally, by an invariably invisible triangle of lights at each end – 10/10ths cloud at about 8000 ft and a ground haze up to 1000 ft effectively cancelled out any idea of maintaining position.

'Having already warned Control that conditions were deteriorating, I felt fully justified in calling the whole thing off and repeating my request to be allowed to return to base, the first occasion in which I had done so having been turned down by higher authority. I might just as well have not wasted my time. My radio decided to go on strike, because whilst I could hear with ever-decreasing clarity the Controller's ever-increasing concern for my well-being, he could hear nothing. For me, very lost and very lonely, it was a very unsatisfactory state of affairs. After flying around for something like an hour on highly inaccurate reciprocal courses, I heard a faint and frantic voice suggest that I steer south as there was some suggestion of a plot north of base. It soon became obvious that it must have been some other sucker.

'By this time I had quite naturally lost faith in relying on communications with the ground, and resigned myself to putting in further night-flying practice in the optimistic hope of benefiting therefrom at a later date. Careful engine-handling enabled me to prolong the agony for a total of three-and-a-quarter hours. Not wanting to hasten my extinction by trying to crash land left me with only one alternative – which I took. Before doing so, however, I ineffectively tried to get my own back with a final crack at the Controller.

'So far as I know, nobody heard my "Baling out: listening out". Perhaps it was just as well.'

Meanwhile, Luftwaffe units were completing their move into new bases in France, Holland and Belgium in readiness for the impending onslaught on Great Britain. Before describing the Spitfire's crucial part in that battle, however, we shall look at some of the modifications made in the light of its initial experience in combat.

No 610 'County of Chester' Sqn Mark IAs out on a Channel convoy patrol from Gravesend in early June 1940. The unit had seen much action over France following its posting to Biggin Hill from Prestwick on 10 May, and lessons learned in combat are reflected in the loose line-astern formations flown by two of the three sections seen in this view

'Aces High!' Six early Spitfire aces salute H M King George VI after receiving awards on Thursday, 27 June 1940, at RAF Hornchurch following operations over Dunkirk. Left to right, Plt Off J L Allen (No 54 Sqn); Flt Lt R R S Tuck (No 92 Sqn), Flt Lt A C Deere (No 54 Sqn), Flt Lt A G Malan (No 74 Sqn) and Sqn Ldr J A Leathart (No 54 Sqn). All bar 'Johnny' Allen (7 and 1 shared and 5 unconfirmed) survived the war, the former being killed on 24 July 1940 when his damaged Spitfire (R6812 – shot up by a Bf 109 from Stab III./JG 26) stalled and crashed on finals just short of Manston

IMPROVING THE BREED

From the time the Spitfire entered service in the autumn of 1938, the fighter underwent continuous modification aimed at enhancing its usefulness as a combat aircraft. In this chapter we examine the more important of the changes, and observe their effect on the fighter's operational capability.

Improved Airscrews

Spitfires of the initial production batch were fitted with a two-bladed fixed-pitch wooden airscrew. The 78th and subsequent production machines were fitted with de Havilland three-bladed two-pitch metal airscrew. Although the new airscrew weighed more than four times as much as the wooden two-blader (350 lbs compared with 83 lbs), the improvement in performance was substantial. The take-off run in still air was reduced from 420 yards to 320 yards, the maximum speed at 20,000 ft increased from 361 mph to 365 mph and the service ceiling increased from 31,000 to 34,400 ft.

Shortly before the Battle of Britain a further type of airscrew was introduced for frontline Spitfires – the three-bladed constant speed propeller. Working in conjunction with a constant speed unit fitted to the engine, this allowed the blade pitch to be adjusted automatically to correct for variations in engine power and speed. Thus, the propeller operated at the most efficient setting for any given combination of rpm, boost and airspeed. Two separate types of constant speed airscrew were fitted to the Mark I and Mark II Spitfires, one manufactured by the Rotol Company and the other by de Havilland. The constant speed airscrews were even heavier than the two-pitch type (500 lbs compared with 350 lbs), yet they reduced the still-air take-off distance

Close up of the cockpit of a Mark I, showing some of the modifications applied before the Battle of Britain. The aircraft has the bulged canopy and push-out panel on the port side, the purpose of the latter being to allow the pressure inside and outside the cockpit to be equalised if the canopy had to be opened at high speed. The aircraft has the second type of oblong rear view mirror fitted to the Spitfire I, plus a toughened glass windscreen. Also in evidence is the thick light alloy cover for the upper fuel tank in front of the cockpit

Showing the value of the toughened glass, this aircraft (N3285), flown by Plt Off 'Bogle' Bodie (5 and 5 shared, 1 unconfirmed, 8 and 2 shared probables, 3 and 1 damaged) of No 66 Sqn, returned to Gravesend with its windscreen shattered but intact after taking a hit during an engagement with Bf 109s over Tenterden on 5 October 1940. The Spitfire was soon repaired, only to be damaged again by Bf 109s whilst being flown by Bodie exactly a week later over Maidstone! Following further repairs it served with Nos 64 and 303 Sqns, before being relegated to second-line training duties in the spring of 1941

Close-up of the Barr and Stroud GM 2 reflector sight as fitted to Spitfires and other British fighters during the early war period

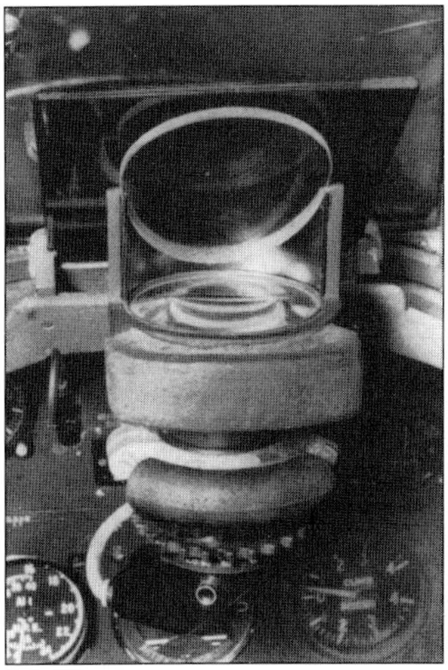

to 225 yards, gave a substantial improvement in the rate of climb and made the fighter much easier to handle in combat.

Armour Protection

Initial production machines carried no armour protection for the pilot or vulnerable parts of the aircraft. Early in the war the value of such protection became clear, but there were limits to the amount that could be carried without an unacceptable weight penalty. To shield the pilot from rifle-calibre rounds coming from ahead, a thick slab of laminated glass was mounted on the front of the windscreen. Also, a 3 mm thick cover of light alloy was fitted above the upper fuel tank to deflect small calibre rounds striking at a shallow angle. Later, 73 lbs of steel plating was fitted behind the pilot's seat to protect his head and back from rounds fired from behind.

100 Octane Petrol

In the spring of 1940 the RAF began using 100 octane petrol in operational aircraft in place of the 87 octane fuel previously used. Engines had to be modified to use the new fuel, which gave improved performance at heights below the full-throttle altitude (16,500 ft for the Spitfire I). The higher octane fuel allowed an increase in supercharger boost from +6 lbs to +12 lbs, without risk of detonation that would damage the engine. A pilot could select the additional boost for a maximum of five minutes by advancing the throttle 'through the gate' to the fully forward position. The emergency power setting increased maximum speed by 25 mph at sea level and 34 mph at 10,000 ft. It also improved the fighter's climbing performance between sea level and full-throttle altitude.

IFF Equipment

Another important addition to the fighter was the installation of IFF (Identification Friend or Foe) equipment. This added about 40 lbs to the weight, and the wire aerials strung between the tips of the tailplane and the fuselage shaved 2 mph off the fighter's maximum speed. The lack of such equipment was the root cause of the chaotic 'Battle of Barking Creek', however. Being able to identify the aircraft on radar justified the slight reduction in performance that resulted.

Two-Step Rudder Pedal

Shortly before the Battle of Britain all frontline Spitfires were fitted with 'two-step' rudder pedals, with the upper step about six inches higher than the lower step. In normal flight the pilot sat in an upright position, his feet on the lower steps of the pedals. Before combat the pilot lifted his feet on to the upper steps to raise his feet and legs, and thus give his body a more horizontal posture. This raised his 'blacking out threshold' by at least 1 G, allowing him to sustain tighter turns while retaining his faculties.

Early Cannon Mk Is

Although the .303-in Browning gun was reasonably effective against aircraft that lacked armour or self-sealing fuel tanks, the weapon was insufficiently powerful against bombers that had these features. The obvious answer was to change to a heavier-calibre cannon, and after examining the weapons available, the RAF selected the French 20 mm Hispano Suiza Type 404. This gun had a very high muzzle velocity and its armour-piercing capability was superior to any competing weapon of similar calibre. Accordingly, plans were laid to produce the weapon under licence in the United Kingdom.

Prototype cannon-armed Spitfire L1007 began flight tests at Martlesham Heath in July 1939. As can be clearly seen in this official RAF photo, all the machine guns were removed from this aircraft. This particular fighter enjoyed a rather varied career, being converted by Vickers soon after manufacture into the premier operational RAF cannon-armed Spitfire – it first flew in its newly modified state on 16 June 1939. It was then issued to various units to test its worthiness, spending time with No 603 Sqn, the Air Fighting Development Unit and Nos 65 and No 609 Sqns, before finally seeing action whilst on detachment with No 72 Sqn at Drem on 13 January 1940 – Plt Off Proudman was involved with elements of Nos 602 and 111 Sqns in the shooting down of a He 111H-2 of 1(F)./122 north-east of Fifeness. Ominously, his guns jammed after just 41 rounds had been fired during this engagement. L1007 was struck off charge in May 1940

In July 1939 the prototype cannon Spitfire (L1007), fitted with two French-made Hispano weapons, underwent tests at Martlesham Heath. With full ammunition, the modified Spitfire was 10 lbs lighter than its equivalent with eight machine guns. However, the drag from the cannon barrels and the bulges over the drum magazines reduced its maximum speed by 3 mph. In other respects the cannon-armed Spitfire handled little different from the standard aircraft.

Once firing trials began, however, the cannon suffered frequent stoppages. In the French Morane MS.406 fighter, were the weapon was mounted on top of the engine and fired through the propeller hub, it had performed well. But in that installation the mass of the engine absorbed the hefty recoil forces. In the Spitfire the cannons were placed on their sides in less-rigid mountings in the wings – the only place there was room for them. If the British fighter was pulling G at the time of the firing, the rounds were liable to misfeed and cause a jam. If one weapon jammed, the unbalanced recoil forces when the other fired made accurate sighting very difficult – see chapter seven for a candid description by George Unwin of flying the cannon-armed Mk I in combat. During the spring and early summer of 1940 RAF engineers devised a series of small changes to solve the problem of the stoppages.

By the late spring of 1940 the prototype cannon Spitfire worked well enough for the version to enter small-scale production. Designated the Mark IB, it entered service with No 19 Sqn in June, but it soon became clear that the introduction of the Hispano cannon into the frontline had been premature. When the squadron went into action in August 1940, the weapon's reliability was abysmal – during the combat on 16th, both cannon functioned properly on only one of the seven Spitfires that engaged. On the 19th it was none out of three, on the 24th two out of eight and on the 31st it was three out of six. Following these failures the squadron's commander, Sqn Ldr R Pinkham, complained to his superiors;

'In all the engagements so far occurring it is considered that had the unit been equipped with eight-gun fighters it would have inflicted far more severe losses on the enemy . . . It is most strongly urged that until the stoppages at present experienced have been eliminated this squadron should be re-equipped with Browning gun Spitfires . . .'

ACM Dowding accepted Pinkham's suggestion, and early in September the unit exchanged its cannon fighters for normal eight-gun Spitfires. The Hispano-armed Mark IB played no further part in the Battle of Britain.

Added Weight

The maximum speed usually quoted for the Spitfire I is 362 mph at 18,500 ft, but those figures related to first production aircraft K9787. It tipped the scales at 5819 lbs and lacked any of the modifications described in this chapter. By the summer of 1940 the all-up weight a fully equipped Spitfire I had increased to about 6150 lbs, and its maximum speed had been reduced to about 350 mph. It was, however, a far more potent fighting machine than the original aircraft.

Enter the Mark II

In June 1940 the huge Nuffield factory at Castle Bromwich, near Birmingham, began the mass-production of Spitfire Mk IIs. Externally, the latter looked little different from the late-production Mark I – indeed, the only major difference was the slightly more powerful Merlin XII engine, which was fitted with a Coffmann cartridge starter and a pressurised cooling system that used water-glycol. The Merlin XII developed about 110 horsepower more than the version of the engine fitted to the Spitfire I, which gave the new variant an edge in the maximum speed and climbing performance when compared with a similarly equipped Mark I. It should be noted, however, that the maximum speed of the Mark II still fell a little short of that of an early production Mark I.

In August 1940 the first Spitfire IIs went to No 611 Sqn at Digby, and during the following month Nos 19, 74 and 266 Sqns received the new variant. From then on the Mark II replaced the Mark I in several units, the squadrons equipped with the former being concentrated in south-east England where the fighting was heaviest.

Mass production of fuselages at the huge Nuffield factory at Castle Bromwich, near Birmingham. This plant produced its first aircraft, Spitfire Mk IIA P7280, in June 1940

BATTLE OF BRITAIN

The Battle of Britain opened in July 1940, and in the weeks that followed the pace of the fighting escalated rapidly. Even a superficial account of this epic action would require a book far longer than this one, and as this subject is well covered in other works, this account instead concentrates on Fighter Command's tactics, its system of 'battle management' and the Spitfires' part in the action on the afternoon of 15 September 1940 – Battle of Britain Day.

Spitfires of No 19 Sqn in the tight 'Battle Formation' employed by Fighter Command up to the start of the Battle of Britain, with the twelve-aircraft unit divided into four sections of three

Classic attack by a section of Spitfires as employed early on in the war. Although the 'queuing up' procedure was appropriate for an attack on an unescorted formation of bombers, it meant the RAF pilots were vulnerable to attack from escorting fighters (*via Robertson*)

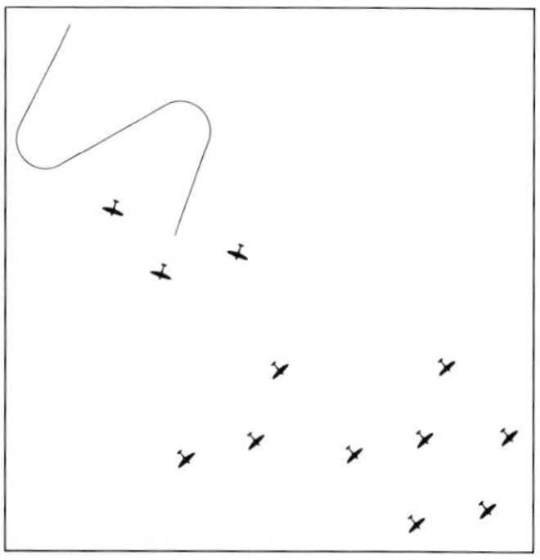

The more-open type of formation adopted by Fighter Command during the Battle of Britain, still with four sections of three. One section was designated to provide 'weavers', flying above and behind the formation to cover the rear

RAF FIGHTER TACTICS

At the beginning of the war most air forces had little idea of how, or even if, their fighters would engage their enemy counterparts in manoeuvring combat. The new high speed monoplane fighters, of which the Spitfire was one, had been designed primarily as bomber destroyers. Speed and rate of climb were the main requirements, with manoeuvrability being rather less important.

Many experts believed that the huge increase in fighter performance since World War 1 meant that a high speed manoeuvring combat was no longer possible. The *RAF Manual of Air Tactics* (1938 edition) solemnly stated;

'Manoeuvre at high speeds in air fighting is not now practicable, because the effect of gravity on the human body during rapid changes of direction at high speed causes a temporary loss of consciousness, deflection shooting becomes difficult and accuracy is hard to obtain.'

War would soon reveal that high speed manoeuvring combat was indeed uncomfortable, fatiguing and generally hard work. Yet determined fighter pilots regarded these as minor impediments, rather than factors that constrained their effectiveness.

During the early months of the war, geography was the main barrier that prevented Spitfires meeting enemy fighters in action. All Spitfire fighter units were based in Great Britain, and Luftwaffe fighters based in Germany lacked the range, or the necessity, to venture close to the British Isles. In Fighter Command it was the accepted wisdom that enemy bombers attacking targets in Great Britain would not have fighter escorts. The notion that France might be defeated and occupied, and that Britain would continue the fight alone, did not receive serious consideration.

For a force of fighters to defeat an unescorted formation of enemy bombers it was necessary to bear the heaviest possible concentration of fire power. That meant placing a formation of fighters close behind the bomber formation, after which the three-aircraft sections delivered a succession of attacks. To that end Fighter Command taught its pilots to operate in tight squadron-sized formations of 12 aircraft, divided

Lull before the storm. Pilots of No 65 Sqn relaxing at '30 minutes available' at Rochford during August 1940. Today better known as Southend Airport, this site was chosen as one of several satellite fields for the main RAF fighter station at Hornchurch

Sqn Ldr Brian Lane (centre) commanded No 19 Sqn during the latter stages of the Battle of Britain, and engaged in a long one-versus-one dogfight with a Bf 109 near London on 15 September. He was credited with 6 enemy aircraft destroyed, 1 shared destroyed, 1 probably destroyed and 1 damaged (*via Mason*)

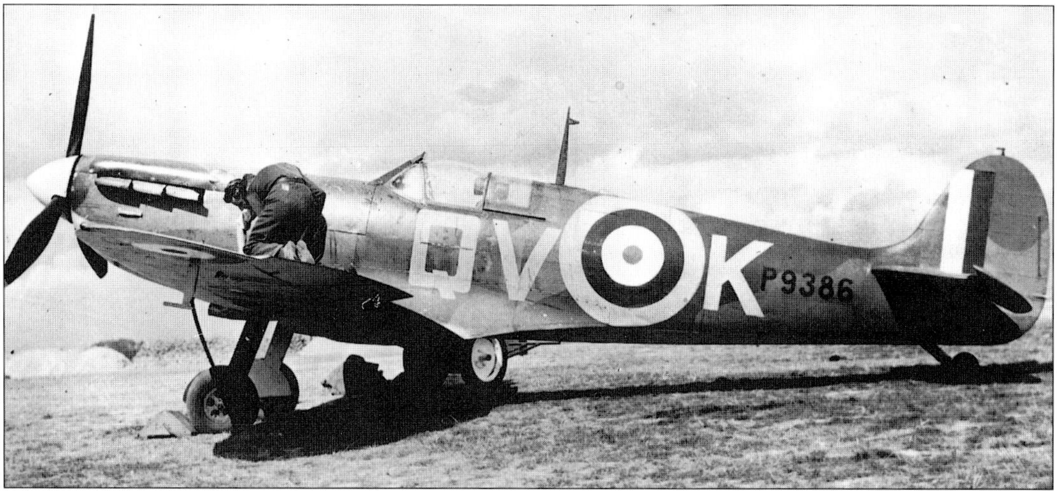

Seen at Fowlmere during September 1940, Spitfire Mk IA P9386 of No 19 Sqn stood out from other fighters of the period because of its yellow spinner – reputedly a hangover from its OTU service. It was a favourite of the unit's senior pilots, namely Sqn Ldr Lane and Flt Lt Walter Lawson, the former using it to destroy a Bf 110 of Stab II./ZG 2 on 7 September, followed by two more four days later. Between these dates, on the 9th, Lawson had also got a Bf 110 (*via Sarkar*)

Non-standard rear-view system, with additional mirrors on either side of the base of the windscreen, fitted to Brian Lane's personal Spitfire I. At least one senior officer disapproved of the installation, and as their effectiveness was questionable anyway, they were soon removed (*via Sarkar*)

into four sections each with three machines. The sections flew in 'V' formation, with the commander in the front and succeeding 'Vs' following in close line astern. The various set-piece attacks were rehearsed until they could be flown with the precision of a drill movement.

Once in visual contact with the bombers, the commander led his fighters into position a short distance behind the enemy formation. He took his own section in to attack and (again in the words of the 1938 *Manual of Air Tactics*);

'. . . (the fighter pilot) stays until either he has exhausted his ammunition, the target aircraft has been shot down, or he himself has been shot down or his engine put out of action.'

The other three sections queued behind that of the commander, and each section delivered its attack after the one ahead had pulled out of the way.

Before World War 2 the Luftwaffe took a quite different view regarding the possibility of fighter-versus-fighter engagements. During the Spanish Civil War that service had learned that manoeuvring combat between modern fighters was indeed likely to occur in a major conflict. For that purpose German fighter pilots employed a novel system of flexible tactics, based on the loose pair or *Rotte*. In cruising flight the two aircraft flew about 200 yards apart, almost in line abreast with the leader slightly ahead – each pilot concentrated his search inwards to cover the blind area behind and below his partner's aircraft. When in combat with enemy fighters, the wingman's main duty was to cover his leader's tail so that enemy aircraft could not deliver a surprise attack. That allowed the leader to concentrate his full attention on delivering an attack on the enemy. Two

Flg Off Leonard Haines of No 19 Sqn who, by the end of 1940, had been credited with 8 destroyed, 4 shared destroyed and 2 probably destroyed. He was killed in 1941

Rotten flying together in mutual support made a *Schwarm* of four aircraft.

Suddenly, in the early summer of 1940 Fighter Command faced an entirely new situation. In northern France the huge Luftwaffe fighter force was moving into landing grounds within easy flying range of south-east England, and from now on the escorted bomber formation would be the rule rather than the exception – RAF fighters could not avoid meeting their German counterparts in combat should bomber interceptions be attempted.

The effectiveness of a combat formation for fighter-versus-fighter engagements depends on three main factors: first, the ability of the formation to manoeuvre while maintaining cohesion; secondly, the ability of the pilots to cover each other's blind areas to prevent a surprise attack on any one of them; and, thirdly, the ability of each aircraft in the formation to receive support from others if it came under attack. On each of these criteria the Luftwaffe tactical formation was far superior to the tight formation used by the RAF. The *Schwarm* could turn as tightly as could its individual aircraft, while the rate of turn of the RAF formation was limited by the need to pivot on the aircraft on the inside of the turn. In cruising flight all pilots in a *Schwarm* searched for the enemy, with each man well positioned to observe the blind areas astern and below his comrades' aircraft. In the tight RAF formation only the leader searched for the enemy, the other pilots concentrating on holding position in formation. That left a poorly covered sector behind and below the formation which enemy fighters could (and would) exploit. If an aircraft in a

This November 1940 shot of No 41 Sqn contains the following aces – second left front row, Flt Lt E Ryder, centre front row, Sqn Ldr D Finlay, immediately behind him, Plt Off J Mackenzie, and to Mackenzie's left, Flg Off T Lovell (*via Franks*)

Plt Off William 'John Willie' Hopkin flew in the Battle of Britain first with No 54 Sqn and then with No 602. In total he was credited with 4 destroyed and 1 shared destroyed, 1 probably destroyed and 1 damaged.

Sqn Ldr Don MacDonnell, commander of No 64 Sqn during the Battle of Britain, had scored 9 and 1 shared destroyed, 3 unconfirmed destroyed, 1 probable and 7 damaged up to the point when he was shot down in Mark IIA P7555 by Major Werner Mölders of JG 51 during Circus No 7 on 13 March 1941 and made a PoW. MacDonnell had earlier used this same Spitfire to claim his final kill (a Bf 109E) near Dungeness on 29 November 1940

Rotte or a *Schwarm* was attacked from behind, a quick turn would place the attacker under threat. If an aircraft in the rear section of the RAF formation came under attack, the action was usually over before another pilot could come to his aid.

Over France and during the period immediately before the Battle of Britain, RAF fighter units were often outfought by smaller numbers of German fighters. Once this weakness was realised, there was no time for a major revision of tactics with the Battle of Britain about to begin. Plt Off Bob Oxspring flew Spitfires with No 66 Sqn during the Battle and was credited with 8 enemy aircraft destroyed, 1 shared destroyed and 3 damaged. He explained the situation to the author:

'We knew that there was a lot wrong with our tactics during the Battle of Britain, but it was one Hell of a time to alter everything we had practised. We had no time to experiment when we were in combat three or four times a day. Moreover we were getting fresh pilots straight out of flying schools who were trained, barely, to use the old type of close formation – they simply could not have coped with something radically different.'

As an expedient, the tight RAF formation was widened out. That allowed pilots to search for the enemy rather than concentrate on holding an exact position on their leader. Also, a section or a pair of aircraft flew a weaving course about 1000 ft above and behind the formation to prevent a surprise attack from the rear. These steps greatly improved the search and mutual support capabilities of the fighter formation, although they did nothing to improve its ability to turn tightly without loss of cohesion.

'Battle Management'

Although the type of tactical formation used by RAF Fighter Command was inferior to that employed in the Luftwaffe, this was only one aspect of air fighting tactics. Another, and arguably more important, aspect of tactics was the technique now called 'Battle Management', and in that the RAF was greatly superior. When a German fighter *Gruppe* crossed the coast of England on a mission, its pilots' knew only what they had been told at their briefing and what they and others in their unit saw and reported by radio. Fighter *Gruppen* could not communicate between each other, thus hindering a co-ordinated response to an unexpected move by the defenders.

In the RAF it was quite different. Thanks to the system of ground fighter control that ACM Dowding had established, the defensive commander could adjust his response to the enemy threat as it developed. Also, he could assemble and commit his forces where and when he chose.

To see how the RAF squadrons were directed into action we shall look at the way the system functioned on the afternoon of 15 September 1940 – Battle of Britain Day. The action was fought in the No 11 Group area whose commander, Air Vice-Marshal (AVM) Keith Park, directed the defensive reaction from his underground operations room at Uxbridge, to the west of London. The table at the end of this chapter shows the times of the scramble orders and the initial instructions passed to the Spitfire and Hurricane squadrons sent to

Spitfire I N3072 of No 611 Sqn jacked up and firing its eight machine guns into the firing butts at Digby. Almost certainly this was a demonstration set up for the press, for it formed no part of the normal checking procedure of the Spitfire's armament. This particular airframe had initially been issued to No 54 Sqn at Hornchurch in November 1939, before being sent north to No 611 the following month. It served with the auxiliary squadron until relegated to OTU duties in late August 1940, having been replaced in the frontline by a factory-fresh Mark IIA (*via Scutts*)

Illustrating the relative ineffectiveness of the .303-in machine gun against enemy bombers, this Do 17Z of *Kampfgeschwader* 76 crash landed in France with more than 200 bullet holes, which indicated that at least two British fighters had fired most of their complement of ammunition into the bomber from short range. On the original print some 50 bullet hits are visible (*via Rehm*)

engage the enemy raiding force that afternoon. The Group's fighter control tactics on the 15th were typical of those employed during this phase of the Battle.

Some publications have stated that No 11 Group sent squadrons into action singly, in contrast to those of No 12 Group which flew in larger formations. The pattern of scrambles by No 11 Group that

Plt Off Harbourne Stephen flew with No 74 Sqn over Dunkirk and in the Battle of Britain. Up to mid-December 1940, he was credited with 9 destroyed, 7 shared destroyed, 3 probably destroyed and 6 damaged (*via Franks*)

Flt Lt John Mungo-Park was another high scoring pilot with No 74 Sqn during 1940. Up to 30 November he was credited with 9 destroyed, 2 shared destroyed, 5 probably destroyed and 4 damaged. In June 1941 he added two further victories to his score, but was killed in action on the 27th of that month (*via Franks*)

afternoon reveals a more complex picture. The Hurricane squadrons went into action as ten pairs and four singletons, whilst three of the Spitfire units flew together as a single wing, two operated as a pair and two operated as singletons.

Another oft-repeated canard has it that Spitfire and Hurricane squadrons flew together, the former to hold off the escorting Messerschmitts while the latter engaged the bombers. As the table shows, in No 11 Group squadrons operated only with units that flew the same type. That made better tactical sense, for it allowed Spitfires to operate to their full performance without having to throttle back to allow a Hurricane unit to maintain contact.

The Bf 109E was the most effective German fighter type, but an escort mission to the London area took it to the very limit of its effective radius of action. The essence of good tactics is to exploit an enemy's weaknesses. Park was aware of the Achilles' Heel of the German fighter, and sought to exploit it. Anything he could do to force Bf 109s to consume fuel more rapidly than would otherwise be the case was advantageous to his pilots.

As the leading German aircraft came within view of the British coastal radars, these appeared on the plotting tables at the various Fighter Command control rooms. At Uxbridge, the controller's first reaction was to order a single Spitfire to scramble from Hawkinge near Folkestone, the furthest-forward of Fighter Command's airfields. Ace Flg Off Alan Wright (11 and 3 shared destroyed, 2 'possibly destroyed' and 5 probables) of No 92 Sqn climbed into position high over the Strait of Dover to report on the strength and composition of incoming German force.

At about 14:00 as the German bomber formations left the French coast, Park began to disperse his forces in order to meet the threat. He ordered two Spitfire squadrons (Nos 222 and 603) to patrol over Sheerness at 20,000 ft, whilst at the same time six Hurricane units were scrambled with orders to patrol in pairs at medium altitude over Chelmsford, Kenley and Hornchurch respectively. When the raiders' line-of-advance became clear, these fighters could move out to engage them.

Between 14:05 and 14:15 hours four more squadrons of Spitfires scrambled. Two (Nos 41 and 92) were to patrol Hornchurch at 20,000 ft, whilst the remaining pair (Nos 66 and 72) were sent to cover Biggin Hill at the same altitude. Two pairs of Hurricane squadrons patrolled over Northolt and Kenley respectively, and single units moved out to patrol over Maidstone and the London dock area.

As the defending fighters clawed for altitude, the vanguard of the raiding force crossed the coast at Dungeness and turned on to a heading for the capital. The bomber force comprised three *Gruppen* of Do 17Zs (two from KG 2 and one from KG 3) and two of He 111Hs (KGs 26 and 53) – a total of 114 bombers spread over an area six miles wide and three miles deep. Their targets were the port facilities and warehouses at the Surrey Commercial, West India, Royal Victoria and Royal Albert Docks. The escorting force comprised some 360 Bf 109Es of JGs 3, 27, 51, 52, 53 and 77. Each bomber *Gruppe* had a similar number of *Emils* flying as close escort, whilst a further five *Gruppen* provided extended cover for the bombers. Five more *Gruppen* flew in the free-hunting role, seeking to engage defending fighter units as they moved into position to intercept the main force.

As the mass of German aircraft headed inland, RAF fighter squadrons climbed into position to engage them. AVM Park fought the action in three distinct phases, his opening gambit, launched soon after the raiding force crossed the coast, involving three squadrons of Spitfires (Nos 41, 92 and 222) which tried to punch through to the bombers (there should have been four squadrons of Spitfires, but No 603 was late getting airborne and failed to rendezvous with the others). German escort fighters blocked the attacks and an inconclusive skirmish developed, but that also served Park's purpose. The Bf 109s, forced to fly at full throttle, burned fuel more rapidly than in cruising flight, and would therefore spend correspondingly less time in combat when they arrived over the capital.

The second phase of the action opened soon after the first, and was aimed at maintaining the pressure on the raiding force. Near Maidstone two Hurricane squadrons attacked the bombers, followed a few minutes later by two more.

For the third, and final, phase of defensive operation Park assembled 23 fresh squadrons – all his remaining units – over the eastern outskirts of the capital. Additionally, there were five squadrons from the No 12 Group 'Big Wing' in the north and two from No 10 Group in the west also heading into that area.

That afternoon the RAF system of fighter control functioned in exemplary fashion. The three Fighter Groups launched a total of thirty squadrons of Spitfires and Hurricanes to engage the raiding force attacking London, and every one of them intercepted and engaged part of the German force. Keith Park chose to fight the main engagement immediately in front of London, where the Bf 109 was at the limit of its radius of action.

A detailed description of this action appears in this author's book *Battle of Britain Day – 15 September 1940*. The raiding force took a severe mauling – of the 114 German bombers that crossed the coast 21, or 18 per cent, were shot down. Many others suffered severe damage, whilst about a dozen of the escorting fighters were also shot down. Fighter Command lost 5 Spitfires and 13 Hurricanes during the action.

The most successful Polish Spitfire I/II pilot of 1940 was Flg Off Henryk 'Sneezy' Szczesny, who flew with No 74 Sqn between August and December. Having already scored two He 111 kills over Poland in September 1939, 'Sneezy' claimed a further four and one shared destroyed with the 'Tiger Squadron'

A section of Mark Is of No 92 Sqn sit waiting for the next order to scramble at Pembrey. Aircraft 'S' (either R6596 or X4069) nearest the camera was the personal mount of Plt Off Alan Wright (11 and 3 shared destroyed, 2 'possibly destroyed', 5 probables and 7 damaged). All of Wright's Spitfires were coded 'S', and his impressive list of kills on Mark Is was shared between just three airframes (*Wright*)

Spitfire N3249 was damaged during a night landing at Pembrey on 31 August whilst being flown by Sgt Ralph 'Titch' Havercroft (3 and 1 shared destroyed, 2 unconfirmed destroyed, 1 and 1 shared probable and 3 damaged) of No 92 Sqn. The pilot was in the throes of completing a night flight from Bibury, north of Swindon, to the squadron's Welsh base when he became disorientated by ground mist just before landing. Although badly damaged, N3249 was repaired and issued to No 602 Sqn in November 1940 (*RAF Museum*)

During his 17-month tour with No 92 Sqn Plt Off Ronnie Fokes scored 9 and 4 shared destroyed, 2 unconfirmed destroyed, 3 probables and 1 and 1 shared damaged. He was shot down and killed over France flying a Typhoon on 12 June 1944

ACE'S RECOLLECTIONS

Plt Off 'Butch' Baker flew with No 41 Sqn that day. By the end of 1940 his victory score would stand at four enemy aircraft destroyed, two shared destroyed and five damaged. With his own unit and Nos 92 and 222 Sqns, Baker took part in the initial attempt to engage the raiding force. He tried to attack a Bf 109 above him, but as he pulled up the nose of his Spitfire to bring his gunsight to bear, he lost too much flying speed. The fighter shuddered, stalled, then dropped one wing and began to spin. Baker told the author;

'I recovered from the spin and as I was pulling away I saw a formation of Heinkels beneath me and in front coming head-on. My first reaction was to do as much damage as I possibly could. I flew across the top of them, and pressed the tit as one came into my sight. I was not worried about the escorts, they were too high to interfere. I kept going straight on. I saw my rounds hitting the nose of the Heinkel at the rear of the formation, and continued my dive underneath it.'

As he dived away from the fight, Baker was suddenly alone in the sky. He climbed back to altitude, searching the sky around him for enemy fighters. Then, some way below, he noticed a lone Heinkel that had been forced out of formation and was heading for home. Two Hurricanes were already attacking the bomber, and Baker joined in and fired off the remainder of his ammunition. The bomber's port engine began to trail smoke, and from then on it lost height rapidly – the He 111H-4 of 1./KG 26 subsequently crash landed near Foulness and its crew taken prisoner. Following the action Baker was credited with one Heinkel damaged and a share in another destroyed.

Bob Oxspring took part in the action that afternoon with No 66 Sqn, then based at Gravesend. One lesson the unit had learned the hard way was the vulnerability of a formation of fighters if caught by Messerschmitts while in the climb. A squadron of Spitfires in a battle climb flew at about 240 mph. Bf 109s diving from above attained speeds around 400 mph, which meant the defending fighters had little chance either to avoid their attack or retaliate. The only solution was to 'bend the rules' a little, as Oxspring explained;

High scoring pilots of No 92 Sqn in 1940. From left to right, Plt Off Tony Bartley (7 destroyed, 1 probably destroyed and 6 damaged to 15 November 1940), Plt Off Alan Wright (described earlier) and Flt Lt Brian Kingcome (7 destroyed, 3 shared destroyed and 3 probably destroyed and 9 damaged to 13 October) (*Wright via Franks*)

'Initially we found that we were being vectored straight towards the enemy formations, with the result that we arrived underneath them with insufficient height and in a perfect position for their fighters to bounce us. We lost some fighters that way. To overcome that problem we used to disregard the controller somewhat, and start our climb out of Gravesend *flying to the west*. When we reached the area of about Wembley stadium, we turned and then set course towards the enemy. That gave us an extra 10,000 ft when we met the enemy, which made all the difference even if it did cost us a few minutes more to get into position.'

Bob Oxspring's unit was one of those that went into action over the eastern outskirts of London that afternoon. Its commander, veteran pre-war pilot Sqn Ldr Rupert Leigh (1.5 kills), positioned his nine Spitfires for a head-on attack on the twenty-four He 111Hs of KG 53. Oxspring and another pilot flew as 'weavers', to provide top cover and hold off any Messerschmitts that might attempt to interfere. Oxspring recalled:

'While the others went in to attack, I was a bit concerned about some Me 109s above me and did a 360° turn to ward them off. I climbed to get more altitude in case there was a fight, being careful not to lose speed in the process – never get caught by the enemy at climbing speed, as that is the worst thing that can happen.'

Leigh ordered the other Spitfires into line astern and entered a shallow dive to build up speed. Then he pulled up his nose and attacked the Heinkels from in front and below – the quarter where their defensive armament was weakest. The other pilots followed and Spitfire after Spitfire closed to short range, fired a brief burst, then broke away. From his vantage point, Bob Oxspring maintained a wary eye on the Messerschmitts. The latter might have been concentrating their attention on other British fighters in the area, for they continued unconcernedly on their way;

'They did not seem about to interfere so I went down after the rest of the squadron and attacked one of the bombers from out of the sun. With .303-in ammunition you never knew if you had hit an enemy aircraft unless you saw a flash or some obvious form of damage. The Heinkel broke away from the formation. I continued on, going down fast, and went through the formation.'

Later Oxspring was credited with one He 111 damaged. Three other squadrons – No 72 with Spitfires and two with Hurricanes – also engaged the KG 53 formation at about the same time. One bomber was shot down and two more suffered damage and were forced to leave their formation. Later, both would be finished off by fighters from other RAF units.

Sgt Don Kingaby flew with Nos 266 Sqn for a short time, then moved to No 92 Sqn. At the end of 1940 his score stood at 8 destroyed, 1 shared destroyed, 2 probably destroyed and 9 damaged. As the war progressed he added further kills, his final total being 21 destroyed, 2 shared destroyed, 6 probably destroyed and 11 damaged. He is seen here late in 1941 after his squadron had converted to Mark Vs (*via Franks*)

Flg Off Bob Holland (5 and 1 shared destroyed, 2 and 2 shared unconfirmed destroyed, 4 probables, 6 and 1 shared damaged) saw much action with No 92 Sqn from May to November 1940. He continued to fly even after his knee had required plastic surgery to allow it to function properly after he had been shot down by the crossfire of several He 111s over Ashford, Kent, on 15 September

Flt Lt Derek Boitel-Gill was one of No 152 Sqn's flight commander during the Battle of Britain, and was credited with 8 aircraft destroyed and 1 shared damaged – he claimed three kills in one sortie over Portland Bill on 15 August

Two peace-time Auxiliary pilots with No 602 Sqn who became aces – Sqn Ldr Alexander 'Sandy' Johnstone and Flt Lt Archie McKeller. By the first week in November 1940, having commanded the unit since the previous July, Johnstone was credited with 7 destroyed, 2 shared destroyed, 1 probably destroyed, 6 and 1 shared damaged. Archie McKellar took part in the initial action by Spitfires on 16 October 1939, when he shared in the destruction of a Ju 88. Just over a week later he shared in the destruction of a He 111. He then moved onto Hurricanes as a flight commander with No 605 'County of Warwick' Sqn and was killed in action in November 1940 – his score then stood at 17 destroyed, 3 shared destroyed, 5 probably destroyed and 3 damaged (*Franks*)

Fighter versus Fighter

The cliché image of the Battle of Britain, portrayed in paintings and films, is of the opposing fighters chasing each other through the sky and seemingly fighting individual actions. In fact, during a large-scale air action it was rare for a one-versus-one turning combat to last more than 20 seconds. That required the meeting of two opposing pilots of above-average flying ability, both of whom were prepared to accept the additional risks involved in such a course. Quite apart from the chance that the opposing pilot might be an actual or budding ace, there was always the danger that a private fight might become public. A pilot who concentrated too long on an opponent left himself vulnerable to being attacked by a 'gatecrasher' coming from an unexpected direction.

After sifting through numerous combat reports and accounts from the action on 15 September 1940, this author found only *one* instance of a protracted one-versus-one combat that day. During the mid-afternoon action Sqn Ldr Brian Lane (six and one shared destroyed, two unconfirmed destroyed and one probable) led No 19 Sqn – part of the No 12 Group 'Big Wing' – to engage German bombers approaching London. Before the Wing reached the bombers, it came under attack from Bf 109s and was forced to break up. Lane curved after one of the German fighters and in his classic wartime volume *Spitfire Pilot* (later republished as *Spitfire Squadron*), he later wrote;

'He saw me as I turned after him and, putting on full inside rudder as he turned, skidded underneath me. Pulling round half stalled, I tore after him and got in a short burst as I closed on him

before he was out of my sights again. That German pilot certainly knew how to handle a 109 – I have never seen one thrown about as that one was, and I felt certain that his wings would come off at any moment. However, they stayed on, and he continued to lead me a hell of a dance as I strove to get my sights on him again. Twice I managed to get in a short burst but I don't think I hit him, then he managed to get round towards my tail. Pulling hard round I started to gain on him and began to come round towards his tail. He was obviously turning as tightly as his kite could and I could see that his slots (on the leading edge of the wings) were open, showing he was nearly stalled. His ailerons were obviously snatching too, as first one wing and then the other would dip violently.

'Giving the Spitfire best, he suddenly flung out of the turn and rolled right over on his back passing across in front of me inverted. I couldn't quite see the point of this manoeuvre unless he hoped I would roll after him, when, knowing no doubt that my engine would cut (due to the float-type carburetter fitted to the Merlin engine) whereas his was still going owing to his petrol injection system, he would draw away from me. Either that or he blacked out and didn't realise what was happening for a moment, for he flew on inverted for several seconds, giving me the chance to get in a good burst from the quarter. Half righting himself for a moment, he slowly dived down and disappeared into the clouds still upside down, looking very much out of control.

'The sweat was pouring down my face and my oxygen mask was wet and sticky about my nose and mouth. I felt quite exhausted after the effort and my right arm ached from throwing the stick around the cockpit. At speed it needs quite a bit of exertion to move the stick quickly and coarsely in violent manoeuvres.'

Lane claimed the Messerschmitt as 'probably destroyed', but it cannot be linked with any known German loss. That afternoon no Bf 109 crashed on land within 20 miles of Dartford, the location Lane gave for the combat. When above-average pilots fought a turning fight, usually they were clever enough to avoid being shot down. Normally such actions ended inconclusively.

Sgt Basil 'Ginger' Whall had seen action in Norway flying Gladiator IIs with No 263 Sqn (he claimed a Do 17 destroyed on 23 May 1940) prior to his posting to No 602 Sqn in July. He flew myriad sorties during the summer with the Auxiliary squadron, and had claimed a further 6 aircraft destroyed and 2 shared destroyed and 1 and 1 shared probably destroyed prior to being mortally wounded following an unsuccessful forced landing in X4160 on 7 October – his Spitfire had been hit by return fire from a Do 17 engaged off Brighton (*via Saunders*)

Eleven-kill ace Plt Off 'Pedro' Hanbury's X4382 of No 602 Sqn, seen at Westhampnett in August 1940. He claimed 2 and 1 shared destroyed and a half damaged in this Spitfire, which survived to be scrapped after the war

BRAVE ATTACKER

After dropping their bombs on targets in the East Ham area of London the Heinkels of KG 26 headed for home. Mid-way across Kent the bombers came under attack from Spitfires of No 603 Sqn and Lt Roderich Cescotti, one of the bomber pilots, recalled one particularly determined defender;

'A few Tommies succeeded in penetrating our fighter escort. I saw a Spitfire dive steeply through our escort, level out and close rapidly on our formation. It opened fire, from ahead and to the right, and its tracers streaked towards us. At that moment a Messerschmitt 109, which we had not seen before, appeared behind the Spitfire and we saw its rounds striking the Spitfire's tail. But the Tommy continued his attack, coming straight for us, and his rounds slashed into our aircraft. We could not return the fire for fear of hitting the Messerschmitt. I put my left arm across my face to protect it from the Plexiglas splinters flying around the cockpit, holding the controls with my right hand. With only the thin Plexiglas between us, we were eye-to-eye with the enemy's eight machine guns. At the last moment the Spitfire pulled up and passed very close over the top of us. Then it rolled on its back, as though out of control, and went down steeply trailing black smoke. Waggling its wings, the Messerschmitt swept past us and curved in for another attack. The action lasted only a few seconds, but it demonstrated the determination and bravery with which the Tommies were fighting over the own country.'

The bomber took several hits but Cescotti was able to hold his position in formation and get home safely. Almost certainly the courageous Spitfire pilot was Flg Off Peter Pease of No 603 Sqn who was shot down at a time and place, and in a manner, consistent with Cescotti's account – Pease was still in the cockpit of his blazing fighter when it smashed into the ground near Maidstone. The son of Sir Richard Pease of Richmond, Yorkshire, Arthur Peter Pease studied at Eton and Cambridge University before joining the RAF at the beginning of the war. In July 1940 he joined No 603 Sqn, and in the fighting that fol-

Like the bulk of the aircrew within No 609 'West Riding' Sqn at the start of the Battle of Britain, Plt Off David Crook had been a peace-time Auxiliary pilot. By the end of the summer he had claimed 5 enemy aircraft destroyed, 2 shared destroyed, 2 probably destroyed and 1 and 1 shared damaged, plus been awarded the DFC. The author of the novel *Spitfire Pilot*, published in June 1942 by Faber and Faber, Crook was killed in 1944 whilst serving as an instructor (*via Sarkar*)

Crook's Mark I R6699/PR-L being re-armed at Warmwell on 13 August, the pilot having just landed following a successful engagement with Bf 109s over Poole Harbour. Crook had downed a II./JG 53 E-4 flown by an Uffz Hohenseldt (*via Sarkar*)

Taken at Gravesend in September 1940, this photo depicts R6800/LZ-N of Sqn Ldr Rupert 'Lucky' Leigh (1 and 1 shared destroyed), the OC of No 66 Sqn from April to October 1940 – note the rank pennant beneath the windscreen, a pre-war tradition rarely seen during the summer of 1940. R6800 was downed by Major Werner Mölders over Westerham, Kent, on 17 October, carrying American Plt Off H W Reilley to his death. The Hurricane in the background belongs to No 501 'County of Gloucester' Sqn

When No 266 Sqn received Mark IIs in September 1940, its Mark Is went to other units. This fighter (X4179) became QV-B of No 19 Sqn. The absence of a triangular support near the top of the aerial mast indicates that this aircraft carried VHF radio

lowed he was credited with one enemy aircraft destroyed and one shared destroyed prior to his death.

THE 'BIG WING' IN ACTION

During and since the Battle of Britain there has been controversy regarding the effectiveness of the No 12 Group 'Big Wing' led by Sqn Ldr Douglas Bader (20 and 4 shared destroyed, 6 and 1 shared probable). At full strength the Wing comprised five squadrons – three of Hurricanes and two of Spitfires. It was intended that the two Spitfire squadrons would hold off the German escorts, allowing the three Hurricane squadrons to attack the bombers. In practice that ideal was rarely achieved, however. Flying in full strength, the Wing went into action against a large enemy force on only three occasions: at noon and during the mid-afternoon of 15 September, and on the 18th.

During the mid-afternoon action on 15 September, the 'Big Wing' was itself engaged and broken up before it could get close to the enemy bombers. Split into small units, both fighter types then engaged enemy bombers and fighters.

This photograph of No 19 Sqn pilots at Fowlmere depicts, from left to right, Plt Off Wallace 'Jock' Cunningham from Glasgow (credited with 4 aircraft destroyed, 3 shared destroyed, and 2 damaged), Sub-Lt Arthur 'Admiral' Blake, a Fleet Air Arm pilot seconded to the RAF (credited with 4 aircraft destroyed, 1 shared destroyed and 2 damaged), Flt Lt Frantisek Dolezal, a Czech who escaped when his country was occupied and fought with the French Air Force before fleeing to Britain to fight with the RAF (credited with 3 aircraft destroyed and 3 shared destroyed, 3 and 1 shared probably destroyed and 3 damaged) and Kiwi Flg Off Francis Brinsden (credited with 1 aircraft shared destroyed during the Battle)

Any aerial engagement that involves a large number of aircraft is likely to give rise to heavy overclaiming. And, by definition, any engagement in which the 'Big Wing' took part involved a large number of aircraft. During this action fighters from the 'Big Wing' claimed 26 enemy aircraft destroyed, including 17 bombers – from German records it is known that only 21 bombers in *total* went down during that part of the action. Following a detailed analysis by this author, it is possible to allocate 12 of the 21 bomber losses to specific RAF squadrons. Nine of those bombers fell to attacks from fighters of No 11 Group, one to attack from No 11 Group fighters and AA fire, and one to attacks by fighters from both Nos 11 and No 12 Groups. Only one bomber fell to attack by fighters of No 12 Group alone. German fighter losses are less easy to apportion with certainty, because many units went into action more than once, and in most cases the detailed records of their operations have not survived.

Each 'Big Wing' action was characterised by massive overclaiming, and later this would lead to an exaggerated assessment of the effectiveness of these tactics. With

Sgt Ronald Barraclough (of No 266 Sqn) and his aircraft at Eastchurch in August 1940. This unit suffered heavy losses during the Battle of Britain, and after only 13 days in the south of England was forced to return to Wittering to re-form (*via Robertson*)

Christened *Kerala*, X4593 was the first in a trio of Mark Is funded by readers of the *Madras Mail* in India. It was issued new to No 603 Sqn on 8 October, but passed to No 266 Sqn nine days later as part of the swap that saw the former unit (in the 'frontline' at Hornchurch) receive the latter's superior Mark IIAs. X4593 was written off in an operational accident in Cambridgeshire on 22 November, its pilot, Plt Off Penketh, being killed in the crash

Flt Lt Denys Gillam flew with No 616 'South Yorkshire' Sqn during the early part of the Battle of Britain. Up to 2 September he was credited with 8 enemy aircraft destroyed, 3 probably destroyed and 4 damaged. He then moved to No 312 'Czech' Sqn, equipped with Hurricanes, as a flight commander – his final score was 7 enemy aircraft destroyed and 1 shared destroyed, 3 probably destroyed, 6 damaged and 2 floatplanes destroyed on the water (*via Franks*)

hindsight it is clear that the five-squadron Wing was too large and unwieldy for one man to direct effectively in combat. Moreover, in terms of enemy aircraft destroyed, the 'Big Wing' was less effective than the same number of squadrons going into action in pairs (as in No 11 Group).

This negative aspect of the 'Big Wing' operations was, however, outweighed by the one aspect in which they were resoundingly successful: the devastating effect they had on German morale. Before the actions on 15 September, Luftwaffe crews had been told they faced only the battered remnant of the almost-defeated British fighter force. The approach flight to the capital, during which the bombers came under repeated attack from Spitfire and Hurricane squadrons, cast doubts on the accuracy of that intelligence. Then, over London itself, the German crews suddenly confronted more than 50 RAF fighters approaching in parade-formation. On 15 September that happened not once, but twice. The arrival of the 'Big Wing' demonstrated beyond any possible doubt that Fighter Command was far from beaten. If the 'Big Wing' achieved nothing else but to force the Luftwaffe to swallow that unpalatable fact, it was well worth the diversion of effort.

Effectiveness of the Spitfire and Hurricane

While the Hurricane's more-rugged structure enabled it to absorb more battle damage, the Spitfire's higher performance and smaller silhouette meant that it was less likely to be hit by enemy rounds. Analysis of the Spitfire's loss rate during this and other major actions showed that, compared with the Hurricane, it was more than twice as likely to survive contact with the enemy.

Analysis of the actions on 15 September provides no clear picture of the effectiveness of the Spitfire when compared with the Hurricane in terms of enemy aircraft destroyed, as often both types shared in the destruction of individual enemy aircraft. Also, the large proportion of overclaims and the frequent misidentification of enemy aircraft prevented detailed analysis of the cause of many German losses. As a general observation, however, it seems that Spitfires and Hurricanes achieved victories in approximately the same ratio as these types made contact with the enemy.

Denys Gillam's personal Spitfire W-QJ, seen at Kenley in late August 1940. The pilot has left his parachute on the tailplane, ready for rapid donning in the event of a scramble take-off. The cockpit door, seen open, carries Gillam's 'flying cow' emblem, whilst its serial (N3093) has been painted over. One of the first Spitfires issued to No 616 Sqn in January 1940, this aircraft was 'acquired' by No 72 Sqn at the very end of August when the latter relieved the combat-weary remnants of the Auxiliary unit at Biggin Hill. Indeed, so ferocious was the fighting over Kent during this period of the battle that the former unit had not had time to repaint N3093 with its 'SN' codes prior to the Spitfire being shot down by a Bf 109 on 5 September – its pilot, Sgt Malcolm Gray, was killed in the attack (see the profile of Des Sheen in chapter seven for more details) (*via Franks*)

Pilots of 'B' Flight, No 616 Sqn, in August 1940 at Kenley. Among the aces-to-be in the photo are Plt Off Roy Marples (far left, standing), Flg Off Hugh 'Cocky' Dundas, a peace-time Auxiliary pilot (second from left, standing), Flt Lt Denys Gillam (fourth from left, standing) and Sgt James Hopewell (seated, centre). While flying Mark I and II Spitfires with the unit to mid-August 1941, Roy Marples was credited with 1 aircraft destroyed, 3 shared destroyed, 2 probably destroyed and 3 damaged (his final victory score was 2 aircraft destroyed, 5 shared destroyed, 4 probably destroyed and 3). During this same period Hugh Dundas was credited with 3 aircraft destroyed, 4 shared destroyed, 1 shared probably destroyed, 1 and 1 shared damaged (his final victory score was 4 aircraft destroyed, 6 shared destroyed, 2 shared probably destroyed, 2 and 1 shared damaged). Denys Gillam's scores are detailed on page 37, whilst James Hopewell was credited with 5 aircraft destroyed (*via Franks*)

Armament Deficiency

A deficiency common to both the Spitfire and the Hurricane during the Battle was their inadequate armament (no cannon-armed fighters took part in the action on 15 September). After that action several German bombers regained friendly territory with more than a hundred hits from .303-in rounds. To achieve that concentration of fire probably meant that at least two British fighters had fired most of their ammunition into the bomber from short range. The German bombers, and in particular the Do 17Zs with their radial engines, were rugged machines. One factor that contributed to their survival was the type self-sealing fuel tank developed in Germany before the war, the light alloy cell having a 1 cm thick covering comprising alternate layers of vulcanised and non-vulcanised rubber. Around the whole was an outer covering of leather. When .303-in rounds struck the tank they easily pierced the covering, but as the fuel leaked from the tank it set up a chemical reaction with the layer of non-vulcanised rubber, causing the latter to swell and seal off the hole. During this and many other actions during the Battle, the self-sealing tanks saved many a German bomber from the fiery end that would otherwise have been its fate.

The alert section of No 616 Sqn scrambles from Kenley during the Battle of Britain. For several months both this unit's Spitfires and those of No 92 Sqn carried the same 'QJ' recognition letters, thus giving rise to confusion both at the time and since!

Mark II P7531/L-Z I of No 421 Flt's OC, Flt Lt Charles Green, photographed late in 1940 at Hawkinge. This specialist outfit was formed near the end of the Battle of Britain to track incoming formations and report on their composition and altitude. It inherited the 'LZ' code letters of No 66 Sqn, from which it formed, but with a square dot separating the two letters (*Elliot*)

Flt Lt Charles Green was credited with 2 aircraft destroyed and 2 probably destroyed by the end of 1940. Later in the war, whilst flying Beaufighter Mk VI nightfighters in the Mediterranean with No 600 Sqn, he increased his score to 11 destroyed, 3 and 1 shared probably destroyed and 1 damaged (*RAF Museum*)

To defeat the self-sealing tank the answer was the same as that to defeat the armour fitted to German aircraft – the 20 mm Hispano cannon. If an armour-piercing round hit a tank it tore a hole so large that could not be sealed. During the late summer and early autumn of 1940, the work to eliminate the problems with the Spitfire cannon installation went ahead with the highest priority.

Unusual shot of Spitfires over Snodland, Kent, on 21 December 1940 taken from the Bf 110C reconnaissance aircraft they were climbing to intercept. Twenty-three Spitfires from Nos 64 and 611 Sqns took part in the interception, which ended in a long chase out to sea. After suffering severe damage, and having the gunner shot dead, the Messerschmitt managed to escape and make an emergency landing at Mardyk, near Dunkirk (*via Fischer*)

Fighter Command Scramble Orders Afternoon of 15 September 1940

Time Airborne	Sector Disposition
14:00	Hornchurch Nos 222 and 603 Sqns (20 Spitfires) patrol Sheerness at 20,000 ft – No 603 Sqn was late off and failed to join up
14:00	Debden Nos 17 and 257 Sqn (20 Hurricanes) patrol Chelmsford at 15,000 ft
14:00	Kenley Nos 501 and 605 Sqns (17 Hurricanes) patrol Kenley at 5000 ft.
14:00	Debden Nos 17 and 73 Sqns (21 Hurricanes) patrol Chelmsford at 15,000 ft
14:00	North Weald Nos 249 and 504 Sqns (21 Hurricanes) to patrol Hornchurch at 15,000 ft
14:05	Biggin Hill Nos 41 and 92 Sqns (20 Spitfires) patrol Hornchurch at 20,000 ft
14:05	Northolt Nos 1 (Canadian) and 249 Sqns (21 Hurricanes) patrol Northolt
14:10	North Weald No 46 Sqn (9 Hurricanes) patrol London docks
14:10	Biggin Hill Nos 66 and 72 Sqns (20 Spitfire) patrol Biggin Hill at 20,000 ft
14:15	Debden No 73 Sqn (16 Hurricanes) patrol Maidstone at 15,000 ft
14:15	Kenley No 253 Sqn (9 Hurricanes) patrol Kenley at 15,000 ft
14:15	Tangmere Nos 213 and 607 Sqns (23 Hurricanes) to Kenley/Biggin Hill area at 15,000 ft
14:15	Middle Wallop (No 10 Group) No 238 Sqn (12 Hurricanes) to Kenley area
14:15	Duxford (No 12 Group) 'Big Wing' Nos 19 and 611 Sqns (20 Spitfires) Nos 242, 302 and 310 Sqns (27 Hurricanes) patrol Hornchurch at 25,000 ft
14:20	Northolt No 303 Sqn (9 Hurricanes) to Northolt at 20,000 ft
14:20	Tangmere No 602 Sqn (12 Spitfires) to Kenley/Biggin Hill/Gravesend area.
14:28	Middle Wallop (No 10 Group) No 609 Sqn (13 Spitfires) to Brooklands/Kenley area at 15,000 ft

Colour Plates

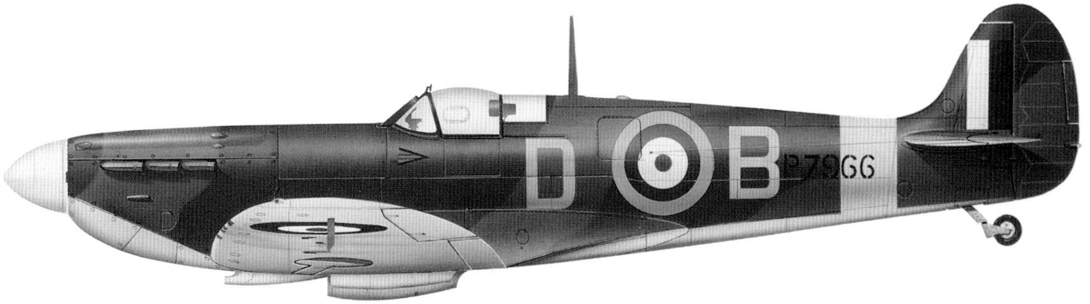

1
Mk IIA P7966/D-B of Wg Cdr Douglas Bader, OC Tangmere Wing, March 1941

2
Mk I K9854/QV-W of Flt Lt Wilfred Clouston, No 19 Sqn, Duxford, March 1940

3
Mk IB R6776/QV-H of Flt Sgt George Unwin, No 19 Sqn, Fowlmere, August 1940

4
Mk I P9386/QV-K of Sqn Ldr Brian Lane, OC No 19 Sqn, Fowlmere, September 1940

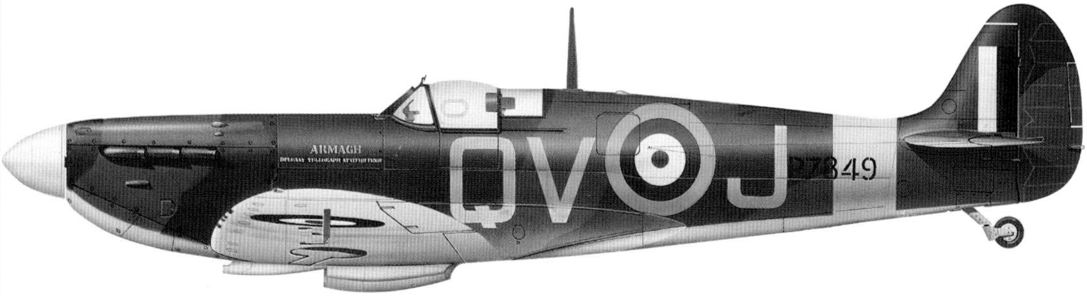

5
Mk IIA P7849/QV-J *Armagh* of Flt Lt Walter Lawson, No 19 Sqn, Fowlmere, June 1941

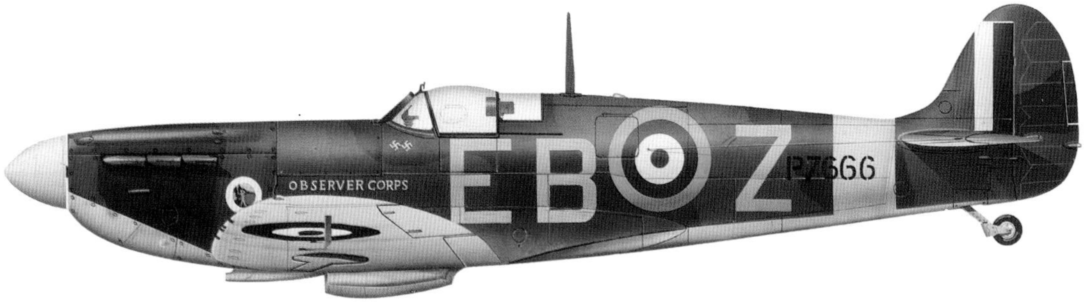

6
Mk IIA P7666/EB-Z *OBSERVER CORPS* of Sqn Ldr Donald Finlay, OC No 41 Sqn, Hornchurch, November 1940

7
Mk I N3173/KL-N of Plt Off Colin Gray, No 54 Sqn, Hornchurch, May 1940

8
Mk I N3183/KL-B *KIWI* of Plt Off Alan Deere, No 54 Sqn, Hornchurch, May 1940

9
Mk I P9389/KL-A of Sqn Ldr James Leathart, OC No 54 Sqn, Hornchurch, May 1940

10
Mk I P9554/K-SH of Plt Off James O'Meara, No 64 Sqn, Kenley, August 1940

11
Mk I K9906/FZ-L of Flt Lt Robert Stanford Tuck, No 65 Sqn, Hornchurch, August 1939

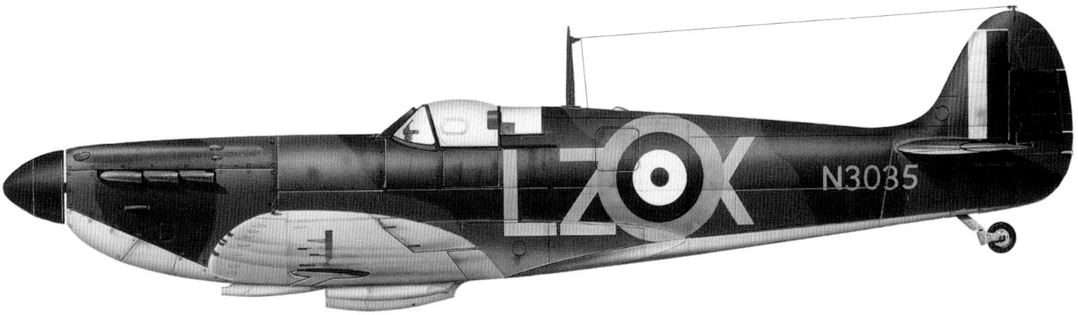

12
Mk I N3035/LZ-X of Plt Off Hubert Allen, No 66 Sqn, Kenley, September 1940

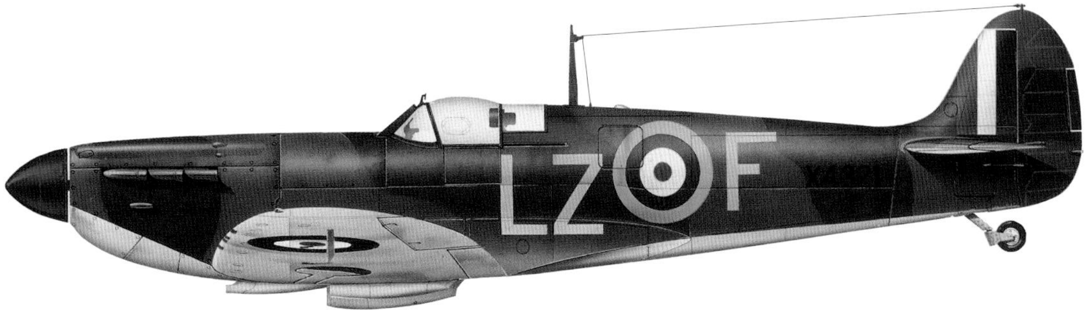

13

Mk I X4321/LZ-F of Plt Off Crelin 'Bogle' Bodie, No 66 Sqn, Kenley, September 1940

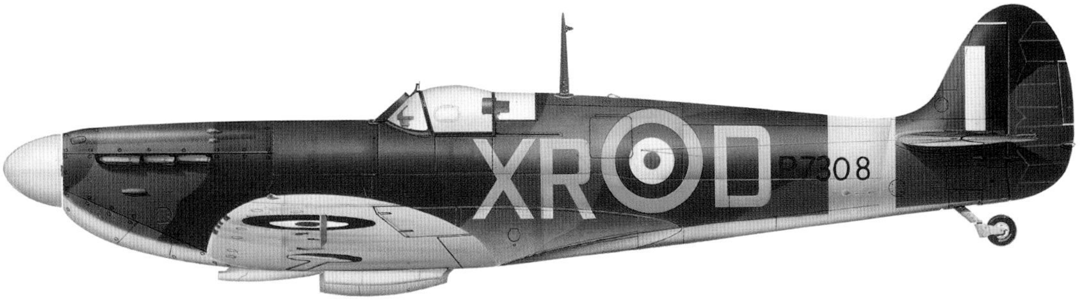

14

Mk IIA P7308/XR-D of Plt Off William Dunn, No 71 'Eagle' Sqn, North Weald, August 1941

15

Mk I (serial unknown)/RN-J of Flt Lt Desmond Sheen, No 72 Sqn, Acklington, August 1940

16

Mk I K9953/ZP-A of Flt Lt Adolf Malan, No 74 Sqn, Hornchurch, May/June 1940

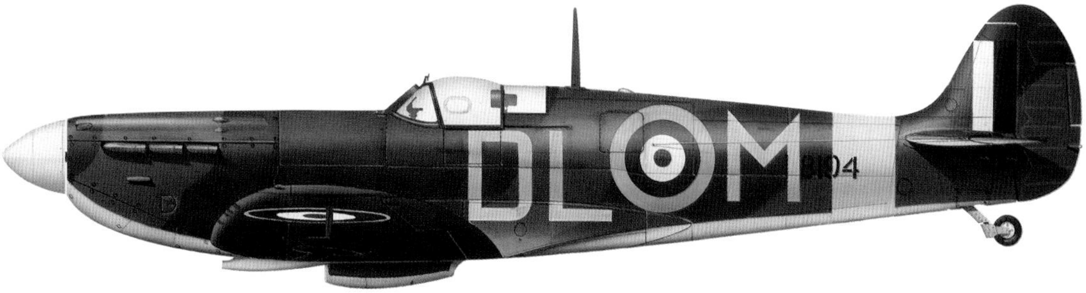

17

Mk IIA P8194/DL-M *Gold Coast I* of Sgt Donald McKay, No 91 Sqn, Hawkinge, April 1941

18

Mk I R6596/QJ-S of Plt Off Alan Wright, No 92 Sqn, Pembrey, August 1940

19

Mk I N3249/QJ-P of Sgt Ralph Havercroft, No 92 Sqn, Pembrey, August 1940

20

Mk IB R6908/QJ-F of Flt Lt Brian Kingcome, No 92 Sqn, Biggin Hill, November 1940

21
Mk I X4036/D-AZ of Plt Off Robert Doe, No 234 Sqn, Middle Wallop, August 1940

22
Mk II P8081/DU-R *GARFIELD WESTON IV* of Flt Lt Adolphe Vybiral, No 312 'Czech' Sqn, Ayr, November 1941

23
Mk I L1004/LO-Q of Sqn Ldr Alexander 'Sandy' Johnstone, OC No 602 Sqn, Drem, June 1940

24
Mk I L1019/LO-G of Sgt Basil Whall, No 602 Sqn, Westhampnett, August 1940

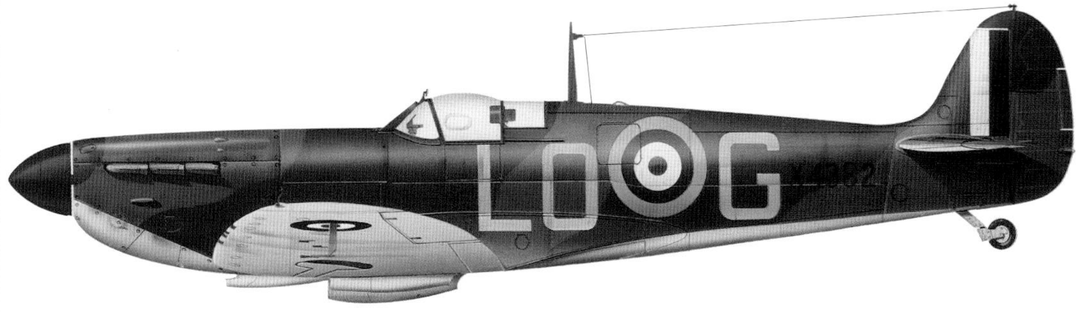

25
Mk I X4382/LO-G of Plt Off Osgood Hanbury, No 602 Sqn, Westhampnett, September 1940

26
Mk I X4541/LO-M of Sgt Cyril Babbage, No 602 Sqn, Westhampnett, October 1940

27
Mk I L1067/XT-D of Sqn Ldr George Denholm, OC No 603 Sqn, Aberdeen/Dyce, March 1940

28
Mk I R6835/XT-W of Flg Off Brian Carbury, No 603 Sqn, Hornchurch, August 1940

29
Mk I X4277/XT-M of Flg Off Richard Hillary, No 603 Sqn, Hornchurch

30
Mk I N3288/XT-H of Plt Off George Gilroy, No 603 Sqn, Biggin Hill, August 1940

31
Mk I X4250/XT-X of Sgt Jack Stokoe, No 603 Sqn, Biggin Hill, August 1940

32
Mk I P9322/PR-L of Plt Off David Crook, No 609 Sqn, Middle Wallop, July 1940

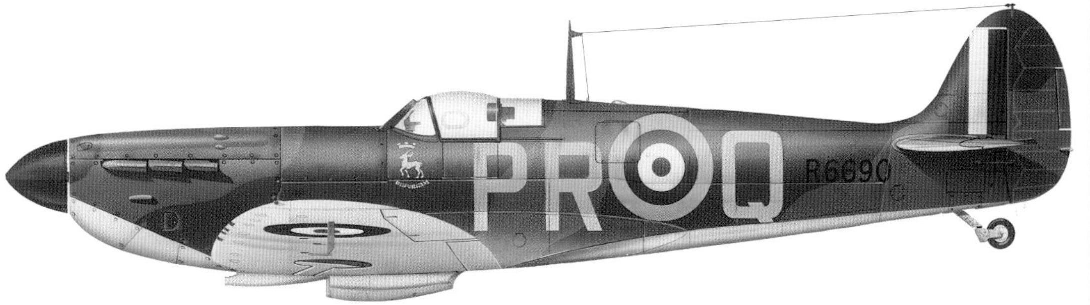

33
Mk I R6690/PR-Q of Flg Off John Dundas, No 609 Sqn, Middle Wallop, August 1940

34
Mk I R6691/PR-J of Flt Lt Frank Howell, No 609 Sqn, Middle Wallop, August 1940

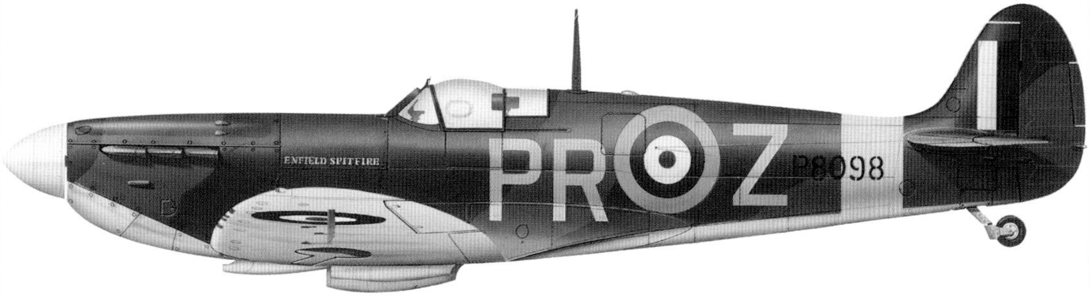

35
Mk IIA P8098/PR-Z *ENFIELD SPITFIRE* of Flt Lt John Curchin, No 609 Sqn, Biggin Hill, May 1941

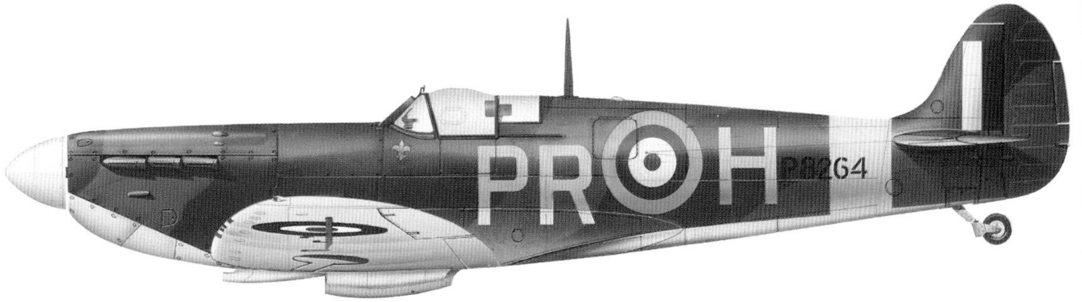

36
Mk IIA P8264/PR-H of Flg Off John Bisdee, No 609 Sqn, Biggin Hill, May 1941

37
Mk I R6806/DW-N of Flt Lt John Ellis, No 610 Sqn, Biggin Hill, July 1940

38
Mk I P9433/DW-E of Plt Off Constantine Pegge, No 610 Sqn, Biggin Hill, August 1940

39
Mk I X4253/N-FY of Sgt Wilfred Duncan-Smith, No 611 Sqn, Rochford, December 1940

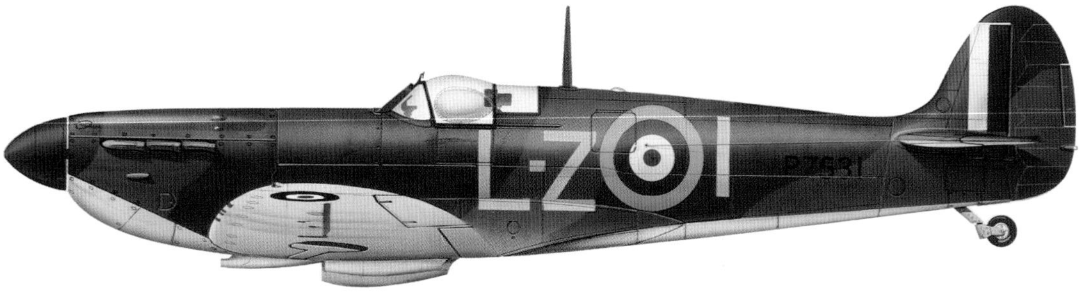

40
Mk IIA P7531/L-Z-I of Flt Lt Charles Green, No 421 Flt, Hawkinge, November 1940

1
Plt Off David Crook of No 609 'West Riding' Sqn, Middle Wallop, September 1940

2
Flt Sgt George 'Grumpy' Unwin and 'Flash', both of No 19 Sqn, Duxford, June 1940

3
Sub-Lt Arthur 'Admiral' Blake, Fleet Air Arm, of No 19 Sqn, Fowlmere, September 1940

4
Sqn Ldr Johnny Kent, OC No 92 Sqn, Biggin Hill, November 1940

5
Plt Off Desmond Williams of No 92 Sqn, Northolt, May 1940

6
Sqn Ldr Don Finlay, OC No 41 Sqn, Hornchurch, November 1940

FURTHER IMPROVEMENTS AND NEW TACTICS

Rearming the Spitfire

Although the introduction of the Hispano-armed Spitfire into action had proved an embarrassing failure, the lack of punch from the .303-in Browning gun ensured that the heavier weapon remained high on Fighter Command's list of requirements. Under a crash programme the faults of the Hispano installation for the Spitfire were finally eradicated, although not in time for this weapon to play any major part in the Battle of Britain.

Even when the cannon did fire properly, there was another problem to be solved – the 60-round magazine attached to each Hispano gun contained ammunition for only five seconds of firing. That was insufficient for normal air-to-air combat. Accordingly, the next batch of cannon-armed Mark Is delivered to the RAF carried a mixed armament of two Hispano guns and four machine guns. It was a good compromise, and in November 1940 No 92 Sqn re-equipped with the new variant. Like the earlier two-cannon Spitfire, the new variant with the mixed armament was designated the Mark IB, and in order to differentiate these aircraft from the Mark Is armed with eight machine guns, the latter were re-designated as Mark IAs.

The initial batches of Spitfire IIs all carried the eight machine-gun armament, but later small numbers of these aircraft were fitted with the two cannon and four machine-gun armament – these aircraft were designated Mark IIBs, while their machine-gun armed counterparts were re-designated as Mark IIAs.

Spitfire IIA (long range) of No 118 Sqn shows off its 40-gallon fixed tank under the port wing whilst parked at Ibsley in April 1941. Initially trialled on the Mark I, the external tanks made their service debut in June 1940 when several suitably-modified Spitfires were sent to No 602 Sqn at Drem for frontline evaluation – they were primarily engaged in performing extended convoy patrols, and never had the chance to fire their guns in anger (*Lambermont*)

Metal Ailerons

A serious limitation of the early Spitfire in combat was that if it exceeded 400 mph in the dive its ailerons seemed to lock almost solid, the pilot having to use all the strength of both hands to get even a small amount of lateral movement of the stick. Wind tun-

Spitfire IBs of No 92 Sqn armed with two cannon and four machine guns, seen operating from Manston during the final weeks of 1940. The aircraft nearest to the camera was the regular mount of Flt Lt Brian Kingcome, who had seen action over Dunkirk and during the Battle of Britain. This aircraft (R6908) later became one of the first Mark Vs to reach the frontline, prior to being written off in a forced landing after suffering combat damage over France whilst still serving with No 92 Sqn in May 1941 (*Wright*)

nel tests revealed that the cause of the problem was 'ballooning' of the fabric covering on the control surface, which greatly increased the stick force necessary to move it.

To solve the problem Supermarine produced a set of ailerons covered with light alloy instead of fabric. The stiffer metal covering did not 'balloon' at high speeds, and in November 1940 metal-covered ailerons were fitted to a Spitfire. Pilots who flew it reported a considerable improvement in the high speed handling of the modified fighter, so following successful trials, Fighter Command ordered a crash programme to fit metal-covered ailerons to Spitfire Is and IIs with frontline units and all new machines coming off the production line.

LONG RANGE MK II

The operations over Dunkirk in May and June 1940 highlighted the Spitfire's limited radius of action. At that time the drop tank was still an unproven concept, no such tank having been developed for the Spitfire, nor for any other British fighter for that matter. Instead, Supermarine modified a Mark I (P9565) with an additional long range tank with a capacity of 30 gallons built into the port wing. The lop-sided arrangement gave impaired handling characteristics, however, especially at high speed. With the Battle of Britain then about to begin, the need was for as many standard Spitfires as possible, so interest in a long range version of the fighter waned.

Early in 1941 Fighter Command commenced offensive sweeps and bomber escort missions over north-west Europe. That re-kindled interest in the long range version of the fighter, and some 60 Spitfire Mk IIs were built with a 40-gallon fixed tank fitted under the port wing. Designated the Mark II Long Range, these lop-sided aircraft first saw action during the spring of 1941. Several units flew this variant in combat, in some cases for only a short time, before passing them to another squadron – Nos 19, 66, 118, 152, 222, 234, 501 and 616 Sqns have been identified as operating the variant at one time or other. Compared with the standard Mark II, the long range version was less manoeuvrable, its maximum speed was 26 mph lower, it took 2 mins 48 secs longer to reach 20,000 ft and its service ceiling was 3700 ft lower (see the specification for aircraft P8036 at the end of this book). Nevertheless, since it carried nearly half as much fuel again as the standard Mark II, the long range variant would prove its worth as a bomber escort.

Mark IIB P8329 *Sumbawa* receiving a pre-flight check at Castle Bromwich in April 1941, prior to delivery to the RAF – this aircraft subsequently went into action with No 303 'Warsaw-Kosciuszko' Sqn from Northolt the following month, but was damaged in combat during the first week of July and struck off charge

New Tactics

After the Battle of Britain the rapid decline in air operations allowed Fighter Command to withdraw squadrons from the combat zone to rest, recuperate, reform and retrain. At that time most units used the tactical formation already described, although some commanders had incorporated minor variations of their own.

Meanwhile, the commander of No 74 Sqn, Sqn Ldr 'Sailor' Malan, devised a new type of tactical formation. Instead of dividing the 12-aircraft squadron into four sections each with three, he split it into three sections each with four. It was an important difference, for if the formation broke up, its four-aircraft sections split easily into two fighting elements each of two aircraft. These operated in the same way as the German *Rotte*. Malan believed, rightly, that a three-aircraft fighting unit contained one aircraft too many, while a fighter flying alone in the combat area was potentially a sitting duck. In Malan's new formation the three section leaders flew in a widely-spaced 'V', with the rest of their sections in line astern behind them.

On each of the three criteria for an effective fighter formation – manoeuvrability with cohesion, coverage of blind areas and mutual support – Malan's formation was a great improvement over that used previously in Fighter Command. The loose line-astern formation was easy to fly, it allowed pilots to devote much of their time to searching for the enemy, and they were well positioned to cover each others' blind areas. The value of the new formation was quickly recognised, and with the switch to offensive operations in 1941, it became the normal combat formation in use.

'Sailor' Malan also produced the famous *Ten Rules of Air Fighting*, which encapsulated the essentials of air combat and were distributed throughout Fighter Command. They deserve to be repeated here;

1. Wait until you see the whites of his eyes. Fire short bursts of one or two seconds, and only when your sights are definitely 'ON'.
2. Whilst shooting, think of nothing else, brace the whole of your body, have both hands on the stick, concentrate on your ring sight.
3. Always keep a sharp lookout. 'Keep your finger out!'
4. Height gives *You* the initiative.
5. Always turn and face the attack.
6. Make your decisions promptly. It is better to act quickly even though your tactics are not the best.
7. Never fly straight and level for more than 30 seconds in the combat area.
8. When diving to attack the enemy, always leave a proportion of your formation above to act as top guard.
9. 'Initiative', 'Aggression', 'Air Discipline' and 'Teamwork' are all words that 'Mean' something in air fighting.
10. Go in quickly – Punch hard – Get out!

Prewar fighter pilot Sqn Ldr Adolf 'Sailor' Malan (a South African) became a leading tactical thinker in Fighter Command following his experiences in combat in 1940. Formerly a flight commander with No 74 Sqn, he was given command of the unit during the height of the Battle of Britain in August 1940, and by 1 March 1941 he had been credited with 15 enemy aircraft destroyed, 6 shared destroyed, 2 probably destroyed and 7 damaged. His final victory score was 27 enemy aircraft destroyed, 7 shared destroyed, 3 probably destroyed and 16 damaged

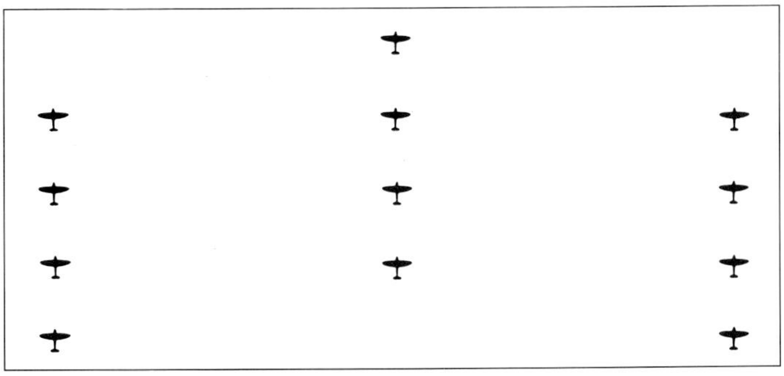

The new type of formation devised by 'Sailor' Malan whilst commanding No 74 Sqn, and soon adopted by several other Fighter Command units. The twelve-aircraft squadron was divided into three sections of four. When the action was joined, the four-fighter sections would split easily into two-aircraft elements

OVER TO THE OFFENSIVE

At the end of 1940 the new C-in-C Fighter Command, ACM Sir Sholto Douglas, saw an opportunity for his day fighter units to adopt a more offensive posture than previously. The aim, as he termed it, was to have them 'leaning forward into France'.

The change in policy came about in steps. On 20 December Flt Lt George Christie and Plt Off 'Bogle' Bodie of No 66 Sqn, both credited with more than five victories, strafed ground targets at Le Touquet airfield. The fighters encountered no opposition and both returned safely – it was the first time Spitfire fighters had operated over France since the end of the Dunkirk evacuation in the previous June.

On 9 January 1941 three squadrons of Spitfire Is (Nos 65, 145 and 610) flew an offensive sweep at high altitude over northern France. Again the defenders chose not to react and the aircraft all returned safely. The lesson from the two offensive missions was clear enough – sweeps made by fighters alone were not going to do much damage.

As Fighter Command's offensive sweeps got into full swing, more and more Hurricane units from 1940 transitioned to Spitfires. One such unit was No 501 'County of Gloucester' Sqn, who swapped its worn out Hurricane Is for the equally battle tired Spitfire Is seen in this June 1941 photo. After completing its conversion training at Colerne, near Bath, the unit moved to Chilbolton, east of Winchester, in order to be closer to the action. Little activity was experienced by the unit in its period with the Mark I, however, and things only 'hotted up' with the arrival of Mark IIs in late June (*via Robertson*)

A young sergeant pilot by the name of James 'Ginger' Lacey (28 destroyed, 5 probables and 9 damaged) had been No 501 Sqn's most successful pilot throughout 1940. Commissioned just as the unit began to receive Spitfires in April 1941, Lacey continued to score freely on his new mount, claiming four destroyed and one damaged during No 501 Sqn's first fortnight in action at Chilbolton. This shot was taken soon after the scoring spree had ended, and shows a newly promoted Flt Lt Lacey wearing a scarf and parachute presented to him by AOC No 10 Group AVM Sir C J Quintin Brand on behalf of the factory that made the items in Australia

Mark II (P8194/*Gold Coast I*) was flown by Flt Lt Don McKay (14 destroyed, 1 unconfirmed destroyed and 4 damaged) of No 91 Sqn during early 1941. Formed from No 421 Flt, the unit was originally intended to operate in the same role as its predecessor, but when expected daylight attacks failed to materialise, it reverted to the normal day fighter role (*via Scutts*)

This photo of the combat veterans of No 602 Sqn, taken at Westhampnett in November 1940, makes for an interesting comparison with the group shot of the unit seen on page 16. Aces McDowell, Lyall, Barthropp, Niven, Boyd and Johnstone are all visible in this view

The Luftwaffe could afford to ignore them, just as Fighter Command had during the Battle of Britain.

—Operations Start—

On the following day the RAF launched a more ambitious attempt to draw the German fighters into action. That operation, code-named 'Circus', involved six Blenheims which bombed an ammunition dump near Calais from 12,000 ft. Supporting the raiders were seven squadrons of Spitfires and four of Hurricanes, for a total of 103 fighters. Hurricanes furnished the close-escort, forward support and part of the target support for the bombers, whilst one squadron of Spitfire Is (No 610) also assisted with the target support. Three squadrons of Mark IIs (Nos 41, 64 and 611) provided top cover for the force, and Nos 66 and 74 Sqns with Mark IIs, and No 92 Sqn with cannon-armed Spitfire IBs, covered the withdrawal.

The bombers completed their attack without loss and headed for home. In the scrappy fighter-versus-fighter actions that followed, however, the Luftwaffe came out the better – one Hurricane was shot down, its pilot being rescued from the sea, one Spitfire crashed and was wrecked making an emergency landing at Detling, and two others returned with battle damage. The German fighter force suffered no losses.

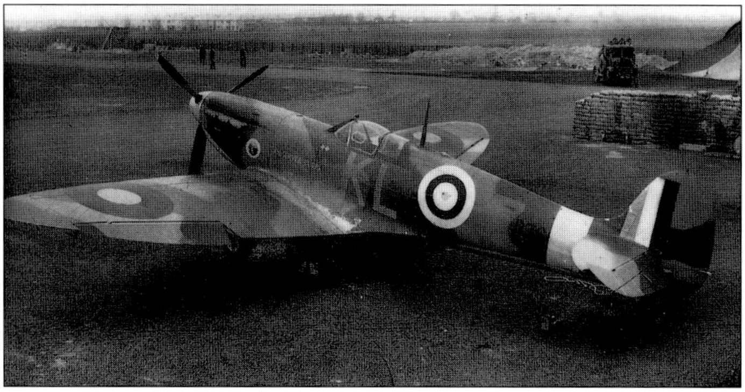

Mark II P7618 was an early production aircraft presented by the Observer Corps (although never recorded in MoS documentation as having been officially a 'presentation' Spitfire) to the RAF. Issued fresh from Castle Bromwich to No 41 Sqn at Hornchurch in November 1941, this fighter served as OC Sqn Ldr Don Findlay's personal mount (it bears his two victory markings on the fuselage) until the unit was replaced at the Essex station in February 1941 by No 54 Sqn. The latter unit received the Mark IIs in place of its ageing Mark Is as part of the swap with No 41 Sqn, hence the odd mix of the former's 'KL' codes and Findlay's score. P7618's service with No 54 Sqn was very brief, as it was transferred south to No 74 Sqn at Gravesend in mid-February, and then lost during a patrol on the 24th of the month – Battle of Britain pilot Sgt Neil 'Jock' Morrison was killed in the crash (*via Robertson*)

During the early months of the new campaign the Circus operations followed this general pattern, although with a steadily rising proportion of Spitfire IIs in the escort – take Circus No 5, flown on 26 February against the harbour installations at Calais, for example. Twelve Blenheims bombed from 17,000 ft, the close escort comprising two squadrons of Hurricanes and No 303 Sqn with Spitfire Is. The high cover wing comprised three Spitfire squadrons – No 74 with Mark IIs at 24,000 ft, and No 609 Sqn with Mark IIs and No 92 Sqn with Mark VBs at 26,000 ft. The demonstration of air power was sufficient to deter the German fighter force on this occasion, and the bombers and their escorts completed their attack and withdrew without loss. Twenty minutes behind the main formation came the Spitfire IIs of Nos 54 and 64 Sqns, making a sweep between Dover and Cap Gris Nez at 28,000 ft to engage enemy fighters drawn up by the earlier incursion. During a brief skirmish with Messerschmitts No 54 Sqn lost a Spitfire.

Circus No 5 was one of the last to involve Hurricanes, and it was one of the first in which Spitfire Mk Vs took part. This new variant was superior in performance to either of its predecessors, and was now in full production. By the end of May 1941 eight squadrons had re-equipped, all based in south-eastern England for air defence and Circus operations.

As with the Bf 109 during the Battle of Britain, in its basic form the Spitfire lacked the range to be very effective as an escort fighter. To overcome this problem a few squadrons received the Mark II Long Range variant, with an extra 40-gallon fuel tank attached under the

Seen here at Kirton-in-Lindsey, No 65 Sqn Mark II P8147 bore the presentation name *City of Norwich* on the port side of its fuselage. The Spitfire served with the unit from April to August 1941, then with Nos 308 'City of Krakow' and 350 'Belgian' Sqns. Despite serving with three frontline units, it never once fired its guns in anger. P8147 then served with second-line units until being stuck off charge at the end of 1944 (*via Robertson*)

Mark II P7753/*Pampero I* of No 616 Sqn, based at Tangmere in the spring of 1941. Note that the unit still used the same 'QJ' recognition letters as No 92 Sqn, the problem of the two units using the same codes not being resolved until later in the war when No 616 Sqn changed to 'YQ' code letters. This aircraft was paid for by the British community in Buenos Aries, and had served with No 65 Sqn for a month prior to the unit being relieved at the Sussex station by No 616 Sqn in February 1941. P7753 was lost following combat with a Ju 88 low over the Channel on the morning of 5 May 1941, its pilot, Battle of Britain veteran Plt Off Lionel Casson, being forced to bale out when the fighter's engine caught fire (*via Saunders*)

port wing. Among the first units to go into action with this lop-sided variant in the spring of 1941 were Nos 152 and 222 Sqns. Carrying nearly half as much fuel again as the standard Mark II, the long range variant of the Spitfire could penetrate more deeply into enemy territory. That advantage brought a cost in other aspects of performance, however. This variant was no faster than the Hurricane Mk I, and its climbing performance was even worse.

Although during 1941 the bulk of the Spitfire fighter force re-equipped with Mark Vs, the Mark II in its standard and long-range

Presentation Mark II P8098/PR-Z and its pilot, Australian Flt Lt Johnnie Curchin (8 and 4 shared destroyed, 1 shared unconfirmed destroyed, 1 probable and 1 damaged). Generally considered by his peers to be one of the best pilots ever to fly with No 609 Sqn, Curchin enjoyed great success during the Battle of Britain. Promoted to command B Flight in April 1940, Curchin claimed a further 1.5 kills in Spitfire IIs before being killed in a collision with a Bf 109F-2 of Stab./JG 53 in the Dover Straits on 4 June 1941 whilst flying P4272 – his flight was searching for 6.5-kill ace Flt Lt George Gribble of No 54 Sqn, who had been shot down over the Channel earlier that day

P8241 was delivered new to No 609 Sqn in April 1941. It was shot up by a II./JG 3 Bf 109F on 17 May, but following lengthy repairs went on to serve with Nos 19 and 350 Sqns

Mark IIA P8264/PR-H was the personal mount of No 609 Sqn ace Flg Off John 'The Bishop' Bisdee (8 and 2 shared destroyed, 4 probables and 3 and 1 shared damaged), and it wore his family emblem of a green *fleur de lys* beneath the cockpit. This aircraft is seen taxying out at Biggin Hill prior to commencing an offensive sweep over France in May 1941. P8264 was credited with 1 and 2 shared destroyed whilst with No 609 Sqn, both Bisdee and Johnnie Curchin seeing combat in the fighter

forms was still much in evidence during offensive operations up to August of that year.

Cologne Power Stations Attacked

The most ambitious daylight incursion of 1941 was the deep-penetration attack on power stations near Cologne staged on 12 August. During that operation nearly two-thirds of the Spitfire units involved flew Mark IIs.

The attacking force comprised 54 Blenheims making a low altitude strike on the big electrical generation plants at Knapsack and Quadrath. During the penetration, the Close Escort force comprised Nos 306 and 315 Sqns with Mark IIBs, No 308 Sqn with Mark IIAs and a squadron of Whirlwind twin-engined fighters. Three squadrons of Spitfire VBs comprised the Escort Cover force.

The Target Support force comprised two squadrons of Mark IIAs, Nos 485 and 610. In addition there was No 452 Sqn with a mixture of Mark IIAs and VBs, and three squadrons of Mark VBs. Despite the fine-sounding title of this force, its Spitfires lacked the range to get within 100 miles of the target. They were to fly along the bombers' route to a point close to the limit of their radius of action, patrol for five minutes and then head for home. From then, until they picked up their withdrawal cover on the way out, the low-flying bombers were on their own.

The Withdrawal Cover force comprised six squadrons of Mark IIs, Nos 19, 65 and 266 with standard aircraft, and Nos 66, 152, 234 Sqns with the long range version. The latter met the bombers over the Dutch Islands, while the standard aircraft linked up with the force over the sea.

It was a bold incursion into German territory and the defending fighter and Flak units reacted vigorously. Ten Blenheims were shot

Spitfire in trouble – combat camera photo taken on 27 June 1941 by Major Gerhard Schöpfel of *Jagdgeschwader* 26 from his Bf 109F, when he claimed the destruction of a Spitfire taking part in Circus No 25, sent to bomb airfields around Fives/Lille. An early recipient of the Knight's Cross, Schöpfel had been credited with the destruction of 40 aircraft by war's end (*Schöpfel*)

Spitfire IIA (LR) fighters of No 152 Sqn pictured at Coltishall in December 1941. This Spitfire unit had seen much Circus and Roadstead action flying from satellite stations in East Anglia during the second half of 1941. It finally got rid of its battle weary Mark IIAs in April 1942

Flt Lt Walter Lawson in Mark IIA P7849 *Armagh*, presented by the *Belfast Telegraph* Spitfire Fund. The No 19 Sqn ace used this aircraft to claim his last kills on 27 June 1941 – 1 Bf 109F confirmed and 1 probable – whilst on a late evening patrol over St Omer-Gravelines. Spitfire P7813, flown by a Plt Off Cowley, was lost during the meleé over France (*via Sarkar*)

Mark II P7308 of No 71 'Eagle' Sqn landed at Hawkinge with battle damage on 27 August 1941. Plt Off William Dunn claimed two Bf 109Fs destroyed that day, making him the first pilot in a US 'Eagle' squadron to be credited with five victories. During the same engagement his own aircraft was hit, however, and Dunn suffered wounds which kept him off flying for several months (*via Robertson*)

down and several others suffered damage. The covering force lost four Spitfires (two standard Mark IIs, a long range Mark II and a Mark VB).

That summer the relatively small number of long range Spitfire Mark IIs (sufficient to equip about three squadrons) flew in action almost continually. As a squadron was withdrawn from south-east England to rest and reform, it passed its aircraft to the unit that

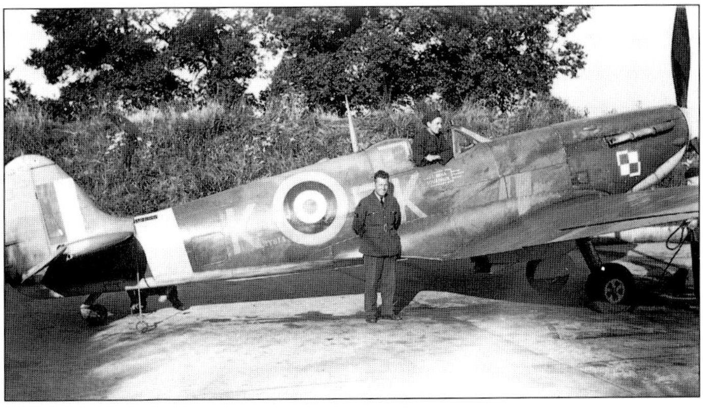

Mark II P7833 *Portadown* of No 315 'City of Deblin' Sqn pictured at Northolt in November 1941. Earlier this aircraft had belonged to No 65 Sqn, and it retained the 'East India Sqn' titling beneath the cockpit. An unusual feature of the Spitfires assigned to this unit was that the individual aircraft letter, in this case a 'K', had been extended into *Krysia* (a Polish girl's name)

The most successful Polish-manned fighter unit of World War 2 with 204 victories, No 303 Sqn began receiving Spitfire Mk IIAs in place of its Mark Is in March 1941. It was heavily involved in cross-Channel operations from its Northolt home throughout the first half of the year, before being sent north to Speke for a period of rest in July. Like virtually all Polish Spitfires, this anonymous machine proudly wears a large rendition of the national flag beneath its exhaust stubs (*via Dr Jan P Koniarek*)

replaced it. For example, when No 234 Sqn moved to the west country in August 1941, it handed its long range Mark IIs to No 19 Sqn.

The attack on the German power stations marked the climax of the offensive support operations by Spitfire Mk IIs. In the weeks that followed several squadrons re-equipped with Mark Vs, and then in September the Focke-Wulf Fw 190 appeared over northern France. The formidable new German fighter had a sizeable performance advantage even over the Spitfire VB, and it completely outclassed the Mark II. Squadrons operating the latter redeployed to areas where they were unlikely to encounter Fw 190s, before they too re-equipped with Mark Vs.

The last Mark II came off the production line at Castle Bromwich in July 1941, and by the end of the year the variant had virtually passed out of service with frontline fighter units.

Already a Hurricane ace with No 242 Sqn, Wg Cdr Douglas Bader was appointed to command the Spitfire IIA-equipped Tangmere Wing in March 1941. At the time he was taken prisoner in August 1941, Bader's score while flying Spitfire Is and IIs was 9 and 4 shared destroyed, 5 and one shared probably destroyed and 7 damaged. His total score, including those credited to him while flying Hurricanes, was 20 and 4 shared destroyed, 6 and one shared probably destroyed and 11 damaged (*via Robertson*)

Aces abound in this shot of No 92 Sqn at Biggin Hill in early 1941 – fourth from left, Sgt R E Havercroft, next to him, Flt Lt C B F Kingcome, then OC Sqn Ldr J A Kent, Flt Lt J W Villa, Plt Off C H Saunders, Flg Off R H Holland, Flg Off A R Wright and far right, Sgt D E Kingaby

TOP SPITFIRE Mk I/II ACES

Note: the ten top-scoring aces are listed in order of their credited scores of enemy aircraft destroyed and shared destroyed up to 1 March 1941 while flying Mark I or II Spitfires. The ranks shown are those held on that date, with their final ranks where applicable given in parentheses.

Flg Off (Flt Lt) Eric Stanley Lock

Born in Bayston Hill, Shropshire, Eric Lock joined the RAFVR in 1939. On completion of his flying training in August 1940 he was posted to No 41 Sqn, then based at Catterick. He went into action soon afterwards on 15 August against the German attack on north-east England when he shot down a Bf 110. His unit then moved to Hornchurch and was involved in heavy fighting over south-east England, during which time Lock's victory tally rose rapidly. In October 1940 he was awarded the DFC and by 17 November his score had reached 23 enemy aircraft destroyed and 8 probably destroyed. On that day he was shot down and suffered serious injuries to his right arm and both legs, his aircraft having crash-landed on Martlesham Heath, trapping him in his cockpit for two hours before he could be freed.

Lock remained in hospital until May 1941. Following a short course of refresher flying he returned to operations in July 1941, serving as a flight commander on No 611 Sqn, then flying Spitfire Vs. He added three further victories to his score, but on 3 August he failed to

Plt Off Eric Lock flew with No 41 Sqn during the Battle of Britain and became the top scoring Spitfire pilot of that action. By 17 November 1940 he had been credited with 23 enemy aircraft destroyed and 8 probably destroyed. On that day he claimed a further two JG 54 Bf 109Es shot down off Clacton, but was in turn hit by a fleeing *Emil* from the same *Gruppe* and suffered serious injuries in the subsequent crash landing – he remained in hospital until the following June. In the summer of 1941 he resumed operational flying and added three further victories to his score before being posted missing in action a few weeks later. Pictured in his No 611 Sqn Mark V at Hornchurch shortly before his last flight, Lock is seen wearing a captured German life jacket (*via Franks*)

return from a fighter sweep over France, and was posted as missing in action.

Flt Lt (Grp Capt) Colin Falkland Gray

Born in Christchurch, New Zealand, he joined the RAF in 1938. After completing his flying training he was posted to No 54 Sqn in November 1939, flying Spitfire Is. Gray first saw action during the operations to cover the Dunkirk evacuation, and his first confirmed victory was a Bf 109 shot down near Gravelines on 25 May 1940 (described in detail in chapter one). During the intensive air fighting of the next few months he was frequently in action, and on 15 August was awarded the DFC. Early in September Gray's unit was withdrawn from action, with his score standing at 16 enemy aircraft destroyed and 1 probably destroyed. Gray saw little further action until June 1941, by which time he was no longer flying Spitfire Is or IIs. Part of his subsequent career is described in the companion volume *Aircraft of the Aces 5 Late Marque Spitfire Aces.*

At the end of the war his victory score stood at 27 enemy aircraft destroyed, 2 shared destroyed, 6 and 4 shared probably destroyed and 12 damaged. After the conflict he continued to serve in the RAF, and he finally retired from the service in 1961. Grp Capt Colin Gray died in 1995

Sqn Ldr (Grp Capt) Adolf Gysbert Malan

Born in Wellington, South Africa, Adolf Malan joined the RAF in 1936. On completion of his flying training he was posted to No 74 Sqn, flying Hawker Demons and then Gloster Gauntlets. Early in 1939 the unit converted to Spitfires, and Malan became a flight commander, being promoted to the rank of flight lieutenant. In May 1940

The three 'Roberts' of Blue Section, No 92 Sqn, pictured at Northolt in May 1940. They had all achieved ace status by the end of 1940. From left to right, Flg Off Bob Holland (credited with 5 aircraft destroyed, 1 shared destroyed, 4 probably destroyed 6 and 1 shared damaged), Flg Off Robert Stanford Tuck (credited with 27 aircraft destroyed, 6 probably destroyed and 6 and 1 shared damaged) and Plt Off Robert Wright (credited with 11 aircraft destroyed, 3 shared destroyed, 5 probably destroyed and 7 damaged) (*Wright*)

Plt Off Robert Doe flew Spitfires with No 234 Sqn until early in September 1940 when he was posted to the Hurricane-equipped No 238 Sqn following the removal of his former unit from the frontline. One of the few pilots to score victories on both types of RAF fighter in the summer of 1940, Doe's total victory score during the battle was 14 enemy aircraft destroyed, 2 shared destroyed and 5 damaged

the squadron was heavily involved in the air fighting over Dunkirk, Malan being credited with 3 enemy aircraft destroyed, 2 shared destroyed and 3 damaged, for which he received the DFC.

In the period between the Dunkirk evacuation and the Battle of Britain Malan occasionally flew night sorties – during one of these, on the night of 18/19 June, he shot down two He 111s (both confirmed by German records). For this feat Malan received a bar to his DFC. In August 1940 he was promoted to squadron leader and assumed command of No 74 Sqn. His victory total continued to grow, and by 1 March 1941 it stood at 15 enemy aircraft destroyed, 6 shared destroyed, 2 probably destroyed and 7 damaged.

By the end of the Battle of Britain Malan had established a sound reputation as an air fighting tactician. The revised tactical formation that he devised was used by most Fighter Command day fighter units in 1941, and his famous *Ten Rules of Air Fighting* were distributed throughout the Command.

Speaking of Malan, ACM Sir Hugh Dowding commented, 'I looked on him as one of the great assets of the Command – a fighter pilot who was not solely concerned with his own score, but as one whose first thoughts were for the efficiency of his squadron and the personal safety of his junior pilots who fought under his command'.

In March 1941 Malan was appointed commander of the Biggin Hill fighter wing, then flying Spitfire Vs. His final victory score was 27 enemy aircraft destroyed, 7 shared destroyed, 3 probably destroyed and 16 damaged.

After the war Malan left the RAF and returned to his native South Africa, where he was an active campaigner against apartheid. He died in 1963.

Flt Lt Brian John Carbury

Born in Wellington, New Zealand, Carbury joined the RAF in 1937. On completion of his flying training he went to No 41 Sqn flying Hawker Furies. Following his conversion training on the Spitfire, Carbury was posted to No 603 Sqn to assist that unit's pilots to convert to the then-new type. After the outbreak of war he remained with the squadron, and on 7 March 1940 he shared in the destruction of a He 111 over the sea off Aberdeen.

On 28 August 1940 the squadron moved to Hornchurch, and from then on Carbury was frequently in action. His victory score built up rapidly and he was awarded the DFC in September, followed the next month with a bar to that decoration. At the end of the 1940 his score stood at 15 enemy aircraft destroyed and 2 shared destroyed, two probably destroyed and 5 damaged.

At the end of 1940 Carbury was posted to No 58 Operational Training Unit at Grangemouth, to instruct new pilots converting to the Spitfire. He did not return to operational flying, nor did he add to his victory score.

After the war he returned to New Zealand, where he died in 1962.

Flt Lt Paterson Clarence Hughes

Born in New South Wales, Australia, Paterson Hughes joined the RAAF in 1935. On completion of his flying training he transferred to the RAF on a short-service commission, and spent time with No 64 Sqn, then flying Hawker Demons. After that he was posted as flight commander to No 234 Sqn, which flew Bristol Blenheim fighters for several months before it converted to Spitfires in May 1940. In the early part of the Battle of Britain the unit operated from St Eval in a relatively quiet sector. However, during July Hughes shared in the destruction of two enemy aircraft.

In August the squadron moved to Middle Wallop, and from then on Hughes took part in the intensive air fighting over the south of England. He enjoyed considerable success against German fighters, and during that month he was credited with the destruction of six Bf 109s and a Bf 110, and a share in the destruction of a Bf 109.

In the first week in September he added further victories to hits score. On the 7th German bombers delivered their first large scale daylight attack on London, and while engaged in that hard-fought action Paterson Hughes was killed. At the time of his death his victory score stood at 14 enemy aircraft destroyed, 3 shared destroyed and one probably destroyed.

Sqn Ldr (Wg Cdr) Robert Roland Stanford Tuck

Born in Catford, London, Robert Stanford Tuck gained a short service commission in the RAF in 1935. On completion of his flying training Tuck was posted to No 65 Sqn, then flying Gloster Gladiators. Early in 1939 the unit converted to Spitfires, but in May 1940 he was posted to No 92 Sqn as a flight commander, and by the close of the Dunkirk operation on 3 June his victory score stood at 7 enemy aircraft destroyed, 1 shared destroyed and 2 damaged. He was one of the first pilots to reach a score of five victories while flying the Spitfire, for which he was awarded the DFC later in June.

During July and August his victory total continued to grow. In September he was promoted to the rank of squadron leader and appointed commander of No 257 Sqn, equipped with Hurricanes. In October he visited No 92 Sqn and, flying a borrowed Spitfire, gained a further victory. At that time his score while flying the Spitfire stood at 14 enemy aircraft destroyed, 2 shared destroyed, 1 probably destroyed and 2 and one shared damaged. The rest of his combat flying was in Hurricanes and he scored no further victories in Spitfire Is or IIs.

In December 1941 he was appointed commander of the Biggin Hill Wing, flying Spitfire VBs. In the following month he was shot down over France and taken prisoner – at the time of his capture his total victory score stood at 27 enemy aircraft destroyed, 2 shared destroyed, 6 probably destroyed and six and one shared damaged.

Robert Tuck remained in the RAF until 1949, when he retired as a wing commander. He died in 1987.

Plt Off (Wg Cdr) Robert Doe

Born in Reigate, Surrey, Doe joined the RAFVR in 1938. Early the following year he gained a short service commission in the RAF, and on completion of his flying training went to No 234 Sqn, flying Bristol Blenheim fighters for a short time before the unit converted to Spitfires. In the early part of the Battle of Britain the unit operated from St Eval, then in August it moved to Middle Wallop and took part in intensive air fighting. By the end of the month Doe's victory score stood at 5 enemy aircraft destroyed, 2 shared destroyed and 1 damaged.

At the end of September his victory score while flying the Spitfire stood at 11 enemy aircraft destroyed, 2 shared destroyed and 1 damaged. He was then posted to No 238 Sqn, flying Hurricanes. On 10 October he was shot down and suffered minor injuries, and soon after he received the DFC.

Doe returned to operational flying in May 1941, flying Spitfire IIs with No 66 Sqn, where he added only one enemy aircraft damaged to his score. This brought his total to 14 enemy aircraft destroyed, 2 shared destroyed and 5 damaged.

Robert Doe remained in the service until 1966, when he retired with the rank of wing commander.

Flg Off (Air Commodore) Alan Christopher Deere

Born in Auckland, New Zealand, Alan Deere travelled to Britain to join the RAF in 1937. On completion of his flying training he was posted to No 54 Sqn, then flying Gloster Gladiators. Early in 1939 the unit converted to Spitfires. In May 1940 his unit was heavily involved in the air fighting over the Dunkirk evacuation, and by the close of that operation on 3 June, his victory score stood at 7 enemy aircraft destroyed and 2 shared destroyed – for this success he received the DFC.

During July and August his unit was again heavily engaged, and Deere's victory total continued to grow. At the end of August it stood at 13 enemy aircraft destroyed, 2 shared destroyed, 3 probably destroyed and one damaged. Soon afterwards he received a bar to his DFC.

Deere then served a rest tour as a fighter controller, and saw no further action until August 1941, when he joined No 602 Sqn with Spitfire VBs.

At the end of the war his victory score stood at 17 enemy aircraft destroyed, 1 shared destroyed, 2

The high scoring Kiwi duo of No 54 Sqn during the summer of 1940, Al Deere and Colin Gray are seen here together at an awards investiture in 1941 – note the striped ribbon beneath their wings denoting their DFCs. Inseparable during the Battle of Britain, both pilots tragically passed away within weeks of each other in September 1995 (*via Mason*)

and 1 shared unconfirmed destroyed, 4 probably destroyed and 7 and 1 shared damaged. Deere continued in the RAF after the war, and retired with the rank of air commodore in 1967. He died in 1995.

Flt Sgt (Wg Cdr) George Unwin

Born in Yorkshire, George 'Grumpy' Unwin joined the RAF as an Administrative Apprentice in 1929. In 1935 he was selected for pilot training, and the following year he was posted to No 19 Sqn, then flying Gloster Gauntlets, as a sergeant pilot. He was still with the unit in 1938 when it became the first squadron to convert to Spitfires. By May 1940 he was an experienced pilot, and at the end of that month went into action over Dunkirk, where he claimed his first three aerial victories. During the Battle of Britain his victory score mounted rapidly, and in October he received the DFM. By the end of November Unwin's score stood at 13 enemy aircraft destroyed and 2 shared destroyed, 2 probably destroyed and one damaged.

In December he was posted away from the unit to an instructors' course, and early in 1941 he received his commission. A succession of non-operational posts followed and his next combat tour, in 1944, was on Mosquitoes. He did not add to his victory score however.

After the war George Unwin remained in the RAF, and retired from the service as a wing commander in 1961. A more detailed profile of his operational career flying Spitfire Is is given in the following chapter.

Although not in the official top ten list released in March 1941, future ranking ace Flt Lt 'Paddy' Finucane was already scoring freely by the spring of 1941 whilst serving as a flight commander with No 452 Sqn, RAAF. Earlier, while flying Spitfire I/IIs with No 65 Sqn, Finucane had claimed 4 aircraft destroyed, 1 shared destroyed, 2 probably destroyed and 1 damaged up to 1 March. His final victory tally up to the time he was killed in action in July 1942 was 26 aircraft destroyed, 6 shared destroyed, 8 and 1 shared probably destroyed and 8 damaged (*via Scutts*)

Leading ace of No 609 Sqn, and conqueror of the great Major Helmut Wick, Flt Lt John Dundas (*via Mason*)

Flt Lt John Charles Dundas

Born in West Yorkshire, John Dundas joined No 609 Sqn, Auxiliary Air Force, in 1938. The unit was in the process of converting to Spitfires when war was declared, and by May 1940 he had scored his first victories during operations in support of the Dunkirk evacuation. Throughout the Battle of Britain the unit was heavily engaged and his victory total grew rapidly. On 9 October, when his score stood at 10 enemy aircraft destroyed, 4 shared destroyed, 1 probably destroyed and 4 and one shared damaged, he was awarded the DFC.

On 29 November he was involved in a dogfight off the Isle of Wight during which he shot down Major Helmut Wick, the commander of *Jagdgeschwader* 2 and then top-scoring Luftwaffe pilot credited with 56 victories. Almost immediately afterwards Dundas was himself shot down by Wick's wingman, Leutnant Rudolf Pflanz. Both of the pilots were killed. At the time of his death Dundas had been credited with 12 enemy aircraft destroyed, 4 shared destroyed, 2 probably destroyed and 4 and one shared damaged.

TWO ACES PROFILED

BY TONY HOLMES

PROFILE OF GEORGE 'GRUMPY' UNWIN

Experience of one's aircraft, and the inherent confidence it breeds within a pilot, is often an important factor in achieving success in aerial combat. A quick scan of Fighter Command's official list of leading aces at the end of 1940 reveals many pilots who had served in Hurricane and Spitfire units prior to the outbreak of war, and in a number of cases had completed at least one tour on the monoplane types' Gauntlet and Gladiator predecessors in the pre-war years.

For example, Al Deere had flown Gladiators with No 54 Sqn from August 1938 prior to the unit receiving Spitfire Is in February of the following year, whilst 'Sailor' Malan had been with No 74 Sqn since December 1936, flying Gauntlets until the arrival of Spitfire Is again in February 1939. Little-known Commonwealth aces like Kiwi Brian Carbury and Australian Pat Hughes also saw extensive pre-war service, the former flying Furies with No 41 Sqn from June 1938, until his posting to No 603 Sqn in 1939 to assist the unit's transition to Spitfires, whilst the latter learnt his trade on Demons and Blenheim IFs with No 64 Sqn in 1938/39, before going to No 234 Sqn as a flight commander again on Blenheims just as war was declared – fortunately, the unit received Spitfires in April 1940!

However, of all the distinguished names to appear on the official list, arguably the most experienced Spitfire exponent was an unassuming Warrant Officer – formerly of No 19 Sqn – by the name of George Cecil Unwin, who had scored 13 kills and 2 shared, plus 2 unconfirmed victories, 2 probables and a solitary damaged claim between May and November 1940. This success had earned him a DFM and Bar dur-

Flt Sgt George Unwin of No 19 Sqn and his Alsatian 'Flash', pictured sitting on K9798 (one of the first Spitfire Is delivered to the unit back in 1938) in June 1940. Unwin flew with the squadron continuously from 1936 until December 1940. Flying Spitfire I/IBs, he was credited with 13 aircraft destroyed, 2 shared destroyed, 2 probably destroyed and 1 damaged (*Unwin*)

ing the Battle of Britain, plus made Unwin the leading ace of his unit.

Like 'Sailor' Malan, George Unwin had been serving in the frontline since 1936, flying exclusively with No 19 Sqn from Duxford on Gauntlet Is. By the time his unit was chosen to become the first squadron in the RAF to receive Spitfires, Unwin was a seasoned veteran. This was soon proven when he became one of the first NCO pilots to fly the fighter (K9792) on 16 August 1938, and was then one of two sergeant pilots (the other was Sgt Harry Steere, who also achieved ace status with No 19 Sqn in 1940) selected by the squadron OC to help carry out the intensive flying trials on the Supermarine fighter.

By 3 September 1939 Flt Sgt George Unwin was as familiar with the Spitfire as any Vickers-Supermarine test pilot, let alone a 'line' service pilot in Fighter Command – indeed, in his year-long relationship with the type he had personally flown 15 different Spitfires. It was this familiarity which he took with him into combat over Dunkirk. In the brief, but bloody, struggles that took place during the nine days of constant patrolling between 26 May and 4 June in support of Operation *Dynamo*, Unwin claimed three kills and two probables.

'We had been keyed up and raring to go throughout the "Phoney War", and fellows like Harry Steere and myself, with four years of experience already behind us, felt confident in our ability to meet any challenge with the Spitfire as our mount. Despite feeling that my chances of success were good once combat was joined, I still remember that I froze solid in my cockpit when the first Bf 109 attacked me.

'I could see this aircraft (a Bf 109E-3 of I./JG 51, Ed.) diving down

QV-I, alias X4474, has its guns hurriedly tended at Fowlmere in late September 1940 in anticipation of its next scramble. Already strapped into the cockpit, Sgt Bernard Jennings (4 destroyed, 1 probably destroyed, 1 shared probable and 1 damaged) chats with his rigger about some rectification work carried out on the fighter since his last sortie

in an arc towards me, with what looked like sparks lighting up his wings – I then realised that he was shooting at me, and all I could do was sit there in the cockpit and watch him, I was so fascinated! I was shaken from my stupor when two shells hit my aircraft behind the cockpit, and I took evasive action. Fortunately I survived this brief moment of "stage fright" and never hesitated again – many pilots new to combat had similar experiences, but never lived to tell the tale.

'My first victory was scored on 27 May – the day after I "froze" – and it consisted of a cheeky Henschel Hs 126 spotter aircraft (of 4.(H)/22, Ed.). The little bugger had used his superior manoeuvrability and slow speed to evade a series of attacks by Flt Lt "Sandy" Lane and Flg Off Frank Brinsden, during which I held off looking for enemy fighters. All the while he was rapidly retreating into occupied Belgium, and Lane finally gave up and ordered us to return to base. Just as they turned their back on him he straightened out to fly away and, feigning R/T failure, I dived on him out of the sun – he saw me too late, and despite an attempted stall and spiral dive, I pumped 240 rounds into the aircraft and it caught fire and crashed.'

The last few days of May saw No 19 Sqn continuing to lead daily wing patrols from Hornchurch across to France, the large 50-strong formations of Spitfires usually comprising aircraft from Nos 41 and 222 Sqns, both of which had been temporarily based at the Essex fighter station, plus No 616 Sqn at Rochford, Hornchurch's satellite field. After several days devoid of combat, the wing saw action in both its sweeps on 1 June, with Flt Sgt Unwin claiming a Bf 110 destroyed, and a second unconfirmed, plus a He 111 unconfirmed during the afternoon patrol. His official Form 'F' Combat Report for the latter action reads as follows;

'At approximately 1000 hours I was in Red Section (No 3) when a bomb was seen to burst near three ships off Dunkirk. We formed line astern and I felt a blow in the leg. I turned the aircraft round, thinking fighters were behind, and then discovered that the radiator handle had shot forward. By this time the other two had disappeared from my section. I climbed above the clouds and found numerous AA bursts and a few lone Spitfires. Suddenly, I saw two large twin-engined aircraft, which were He 111s. I gave chase and was joined by more aircraft of No 222 Sqn. One He 111 went through the cloud. The other tried to hide in them, but as they were only a few feet thick he was clearly discernible. I gave a burst of about five seconds from 400 yards and received return fire. I must have got the rear gunner as no more fire was experienced. I therefore closed to 100 yards, and with a slight deflection shot, gave him the rest of my ammunition. His starboard engine stopped and I then left him to the fellows of No 222, having no more ammunition.'

George Unwin added further details of this combat in August 1995;

'As I went for the bomber it shot into the cloud seconds before I opened fire, but then it came back out again so I gave it a squirt, and then it disappeared once more. This "hide and seek" routine continued until I had ran out of ammunition, by which stage it was trailing smoke from one engine. I broke off the combat and returned to base. Whilst filling out my combat report at Hornchurch I got talking to Flt

Flt Sgt Harry Steere was another successful NCO pilot with No 19 Sqn. During 1940 he was credited with 6 aircraft destroyed, 5 shared destroyed and 2 probably destroyed. Like George Unwin, Steere enjoyed considerable success over Dunkirk, although, as related in the following quote by the former, the deadly nature of war was also graphically revealed to him;

'The weird thing about shooting down aircraft was that you never thought about actually hurting the occupant – rather, I concentrated on destroying the *aeroplane*. The horror of war only really struck home following a harrowing experience endured by my good friend Harry Steere when he and I each downed a Bf 109E (Unwin's was a 2./JG 26 machine, Ed.) over Dunkirk on the same mission, flown on 28 May. The Messerschmitt fighter had an L-shaped fuel tank precariously positioned immediately behind and below the cockpit seat, and once hit it soon burst into flames. The pilot of Steere's machine (from 8./JG 3, Ed.) got halfway out the cockpit before the flames engulfed him, all in sight of poor Harry.'

After flying throughout 1940, Harry Steere was posted to No 8 FTS as an instructor at the end of that year. Commissioned in 1941, he finally returned to operations in November 1943 with the Mosquito 'Pathfinder Force', serving as a pilot with No 627 Sqn. Sadly, Harry Steere was shot down and killed over France on 9 June 1944 *(via Franks)*

Yet another Channel sweep safely completed, a battle-seasoned Flt Sgt George Unwin climbs out of his Spitfire I K9853 at Fowlmere in late June 1940. To the left of his flying boot is a rare piece of early-war nose art in the form of a *Popeye* figure about to deliver his famous 'Twisker Sock' punch. A member of George's groundcrew had painted this cartoon figure on K9853 several weeks prior to No 19 Sqn going into combat over France in late May. During this period Unwin flew several different Spitfires on combat patrols across the Channel, although this particular machine, coded QV-H, was his favourite. Indeed, he claimed a He 111 probable whilst flying K9853 over Dunkirk on his second patrol of 1 June. Earlier that same day he had used K9856 to shoot down a Bf 110 over the evacuation beaches, plus claim a second *Zerstörer* as a probable. QV-H had been with the squadron since 31 January 1939, first being flown by Unwin on 15 March that same year. After serving with the unit for almost 18 months, it was sent to General Aircraft Limited for overhaul on 15 July 1940 following No 19 Sqn's re-equipment with cannon-armed Mark IBs. K9853 was then issued to Training Command the following month, and was written off in a heavy landing before the end of September (*Unwin*)

Lt "Sandy" Lane who recounted a similar tail to mine, except that he was below the cloud. We realised that we had both tackled the same Heinkel, and it became clear why its pilot kept coming back up through the cloud for me to take a shot at him – he was trying to avoid "Sandy's" fire as well! We both shared a probable.'

With the *Dynamo* experience under their belts, the surviving pilots of No 19 Sqn returned to Duxford, and No 12 Group, where they spent the rest of June learning the art of nightfighting, as well as coming to grips with the very latest word in frontline Spitfire – the 20 mm cannon-armed Mk IB. The unit tackled both tasks with equally limited success, and George Unwin had the following to say on the Mk IB;

'When we got hold of the first brand new cannon-Spitfires we were more than a little perturbed by the fact that we had only six seconds worth of ammunition to shoot – little did we know that stoppages would restrict us ever using all 60 rounds carried for each gun! To this day, no one has ever given me a suitable explanation as to how these 30 Mk IBs ever passed pre-service gunnery tests.'

No 19 Sqn steadily became more frustrated with their role in the developing Battle of Britain, which was being fought on an ever-larger scale in the south-east of England. By the second week of August the unit had moved to Duxford's less-conspicuous satellite field at Fowlmere, and were regularly patrolling the borders of No 12 Group, itching to be called into action, but still they had to wait. The continual breech jamming experienced with the Hispano-Suiza cannon from the moment the first Mk IBs arrived on the squadron had still not been cured, and many pilots were anxious to find out what would happen should they enter combat, as the aircraft's armament was restricted to just the two heavy-calibre guns – on the evening of 16 August, Flt Sgt Unwin and the rest of A Flight found out off the coast of Harwich. The following is a verbatim transcribe of his Form 'F';

'I was Red 3 with Flt Lt Lane and Sgt Roden. We left Coltishall at 1715 and were ordered to vector at 15,000 ft (which was later changed to 12,000 ft). After vectoring for about 20 minutes a large formation of enemy aircraft (100 approximately) were sighted ahead and slightly above. They were escorted by a large number of Me 110 behind, which were searching. Above was an escort of Me 109. We tried to reach the bombers unobserved but were sighted by the rear 110's (about 30). We immediately engaged and I gave a 110 (of Stab./ZG 26, Ed.) a short burst at close range, and he half rolled and went vertically down. I was immediately attacked by another 110 but managed to get rid of him. On turning, I found

myself presented with a perfect target. I fired all my rounds into him and he fell over on his side with bits falling off. He dived steeply and his tail came off. I followed him down and on coming through the clouds I saw the end of a splash. I returned to base at 1830 hours.'

George also claimed a second Bf 110 as a probable kill on this sortie, and later added the following thoughts on his victories – the first of literally thousands by cannon-armed Spitfires in frontline RAF service;

'I only had one gun operating following my first burst at the Bf 110 formation. In order to have any chance of scoring hits with the remaining gun, I had to kick on full opposite rudder to offset the recoil when it fired – this didn't help my accuracy at all. I quickly learnt that the only way to secure hits was to get right up the enemy's backside and give him a good burst, which wasn't that long in a Mk IB! I got so close to this Bf 110 that I nearly cut his twin fins off with my prop.

'The aircraft's technical hiccups stemmed from the fact that the engineers at Vickers-Supermarine had been hampered by the Spitfire's thin wing section when it came to fitting the cannon into the Mk I. To solve this problem, they laid the weapon on its side, which meant that the belt feed tension from the gun to the magazine was slackened, resulting in the nose of the shell moving around as soon as "g" was pulled on, and jamming in the breech. Once this occurred you couldn't clear the blockage in the air, and with one cannon stopped, it was like trying to fly a twin-engined aeroplane on one engine due to the pull exerted on the fighter from the other gun when it fired!'

Effectively hamstrung by their defective mounts, the unit struggled on in the frontline until on 3 September an edict from Fighter Command's C-in-C, ACM Sir Hugh Dowding, decreed that No 19 Sqn was to swap its virtually brand new Mk IBs for weary ex-OTU Mk IAs from Hawarden.

Ironically, that morning No 19 Sqn had claimed two definite kills and a probable – again Bf 110Cs from ZG 26 – south-west of Colchester with their much-maligned Mk IBs. A formation of over 80 Messerschmitt *Zerstörers* had been escorting a large formation of Do 17s from KG 2, which had managed to hit North Weald virtually unmolested due to No 11 Group's fighter controllers scrambling neighbouring No 12 Group's squadrons too late. The latter hit the formation as they were heading back to France, with Flt Sgt Unwin downing a Bf 110C-2 of 7./ZG 26 – other sources in print claim that this aircraft was a C-4 from Stab I./ZG 2, which was also claimed by pilots from No 222 and 310 Sqns. Fittingly, George Unwin had claimed both the first and last kills (both in R6776) scored by No 19 Sqn during their frustrating spell with the Spitfire IB.

On the afternoon of the 3rd he flew his Spitfire from Fowlmere to Duxford, where he exchanged it for P9546, which had been adorned with Flt Sgt Unwin's familiar QV-H codes prior to his arrival. The squadron was briefly stood down the following day whilst its wholesale 'fighter swap' was completed, but on the morning of the 5th returned to action – No 19 Sqn lost its OC, Sqn Ldr Phillip Pinkham, AFC, during an interception of a large raid over Hornchurch, plus had a further two Spitfires badly damaged. In reply, two Bf 109Es from JG 54 were claimed to have been destroyed.

The following day, No 19 Sqn's new boss, ex-A Flight commander 'Sandy' Lane, was informed by No 12 Group HQ that his unit was to operate with the Hurricane-equipped Nos 242 and 310 (the latter manned by Czechs) Sqns as part of the Bader 'Big Wing'. On the afternoon of the 7th this controversial fighting force was put to the test over the Thames Estuary. George Unwin and P9546 were part of the eight-strong force put up by No 19 Sqn as part of the Bader wing;

'I was Red 3 on this patrol. We were sent to North Weald to patrol at 10,000 ft, and upon our arrival we saw AA bursts and a number of enemy aircraft, probably 50 in number. My leader (Sqn Ldr Lane) suddenly saw a Bf 110 diving down in front of him, so five or six of us followed him down in a brief attack and he soon crashed in flames. I had got down to 4000 ft by this stage and had lost my squadron in the chase. I climbed back up to 25,000 ft and saw a Hurricane squadron going somewhere in a hurry! I trailed them and suddenly saw three separate formations of about 30 aircraft each, with a similar number of escorts. The Hurricanes attacked the bombers and I found myself surrounded by yellow-spinnered Bf 109s. The usual dogfight ensued, during which time I shot at five of them, although only two crashed, both in flames. I then climbed back to 25,000 ft for a breather, and whilst shadowing the third enemy formation, I saw yet a fourth new one arriving. The escorts soon left the area, and I attacked the rear vic of He 111s in the last formation, emptying the rest of my ammunition (about 50 rounds per gun) into one bomber at 450 yards. It wobbled under the impact of the shells but flew on, so I returned to Fowlmere.'

His next combat kill almost resulted in his death, and saw P9546 so

The strain of battle beginning to show on their faces, acting Sqn Ldr 'Sandy' Lane (left), acting Flt Lt 'Farmer' Lawson (centre) and Sgt David Lloyd are debriefed at dispersal at Fowlmere by the No 19 Sqn intelligence officer in late September 1940. The Spitfire in the background is X4425, which was issued to George Unwin as a replacement for X4179, the latter having been passed on to No 609 Sqn at Middle Wallop on 27 September – just ten days after it had arrived at Fowlmere! On that same afternoon, Unwin used X4425 to down his 12th kill over the Thames Estuary – see page 77 for details (*via Mason*)

badly damaged that Unwin had to make a dead-stick landing in a field;

'At about 1600 on 11 September, I was flying QV-H as Red 4 with "Sandy" Lane when we intercepted a large number of enemy aircraft over east London. We attacked from 15,000 ft in a line astern formation, biased to echelon port, and I fired a seven- or eight-second burst at a He 111 from a range of barely 50 yards. Bits were observed to come off both engines, and the bomber went into a steep spiral dive. I did not see it crash as I was immediately fired upon by a Do 17, which I then engaged.

'Concentrating on the rear gunner in the "dustbin" below the fuselage, I opened fire at about 350 yards, and we briefly exchanged rounds, but he then ceased after I had delivered a couple more bursts. Assuming I had put the gunner out of action I closed in from below and opened fire at a range of about 200 yards. I carried on firing whilst closing in until suddenly the gunner opened up again – whether this was the same chap who had been shooting at me before I will never know. Suddenly a hole appeared in the armoured part of the windscreen (we later found the armour-piercing round on the cockpit floor) and I was enveloped in smoke. I immediately thought that I was dead!

'Having fired all my ammunition, I broke off the attack by diving away to port. Thinking I was on fire I switched off the ignition and petrol, undid my straps and opened the canopy with the intention of bailing out. I then saw that the smoke was coming from the front of the engine and realised that it must be burning glycol – which I could also smell – from a damaged cooling pipe atop the engine. I strapped myself back into the cockpit and began to look for a suitable place to land. I spotted quite a large grass field occupied by cattle near Brentwood, in Essex. I carried out a wheels down forced landing with no damage to the aircraft, and almost immediately a jeep arrived, and a young subaltern and two soldiers with fixed bayonets greeted me as I stepped out the cockpit. With their assistance I took the top cowling off and checked the shattered cooling pipe. North Weald was only eight miles away, so leaving one soldier guarding the Spitfire, we drove off to the badly bombed-out fighter station. I knew many of the NCO pilots based here with Nos 56 and 151 Sqns, and with their help I arranged for a fitter to repair my machine the following day.

'I duly returned to Fowlmere with a temporarily patched up P9546 the next morning, having been posted missing for 24 hours – there were no operable phones at North Weald to inform No 19 Sqn of my whereabouts. As for the Dornier, I never knew what happened to it. However, it certainly could not have been in mint condition as I had fired almost all my ammunition into it at quite close range.'

Proving he could take dead-stick landings in his stride, George produced his best combat return on 15 September, a date now immortalised for over five decades as Battle of Britain Day. He flew two sorties with the Bader wing during the course of the day, scoring his first victory near Biggin Hill whilst participating in the morning patrol over south London. The official combat report stated;

'I was Red Three with Flt Lt Lawson. We sighted the enemy aircraft who were in vics of three. The escorts dived singly on us, and I engaged one of them (Me 109) with a yellow nose. I gave one burst of six seconds and enemy aircraft burst into flames. Pilot baled out. Enemy aircraft crashed approximately between Redhill and Westerham. I searched around for half-an-hour but could not find any other enemy aircraft. I landed at 1250.'

After returning to Fowlmere and filling in their respective Form 'F's', the pilots had hardly had time to catch breath when word came through of eight to ten large enemy formations massing over the Channel. Scrambled late from their airfields in No 12 Group, the five-squadron strong Wing struggled to formate and gain height before tackling the Luftwaffe over London. George Unwin takes up the story;

'I was lucky to survive that second sortie unscathed, as through my own stupidity I got separated from the rest of the Wing. We were led through a gap in the cloud over London by Sqn Ldr Bader of No 242 Sqn, and there in front of us was a sight that looked just like a pre-war Hendon Air Pageant flypast. We were at about 23,000 ft and the bombers were below us at 20,000. I was transfixed by a squadron of Hurricanes struggling to engage these aircraft, and I had completely forgotten about their escort – I flew straight into the middle of them! The next thing I knew literally thousands of yellow-nosed Messerschmitts were whistling by all around me less than 100 yards away, so I pulled the bloody stick back, went into a steep turn, and held it there! I gave the odd machine a quick burst as it flew past me, and succeeded in forcing one to half roll and dive into cloud below. I followed him down, but my windscreen froze at 6000 ft and he escaped. I then climbed back up to 25,000 ft in search of my wing-mates, but as was often the case in these aerial duels, the sky had gone from being heavy with aircraft to totally empty in a matter of seconds. After several minutes I spotted a pair of Bf 109s above me flying back in a loose *Rotte* formation towards the Channel, obviously intent on heading home. After a long chase, I finally caught them as they crossed the Kent coast at Lydd, and after firing a long burst into the trailing fighter, it immediately burst into flames and crashed just offshore. Inexplicably, the leader failed to take any evasive action and he too was shot down on fire into the sea seconds later.

'I had survived this mission simply because the Spitfire could sustain a continuous rate of turn inside the Bf 109E without stalling – the latter was known for flicking into a vicious stall spin without prior warning if pulled around too tightly. The Spitfire would give a shudder to signal it was close to the edge, so as soon as you felt the shake you eased off the stick pressure.'

Looking at Luftwaffe loss reports for 15 September, it is likely that the two Bf 109s downed by Unwin were E-4s from Stab I./JG 77 and 3./JG 77 based at St Omer.

Two days later Flt Sgt George Unwin received notification that he was to be awarded a DFM, the squadron diary noting that his score then stood at 10 confirmed kills. He claimed his 11th victory – a Bf 110 – the following afternoon during a wing sweep which was to result in claims for the destruction of nearly 30 aircraft – all for the loss of two No 19 Sqn Spitfires that forced landed with engine damage.

Following the postponement of Operation *Sealion* on 17 September, the Luftwaffe began to scale down its attacks on England,

Anonymous Spitfire IA of No 19 Sqn being re-armed at Fowlmere after going into action in mid- September 1940. Note that the fabric patches that had been covering the gun ports had all been blown away, indicating that the guns had been fired. The armourers under the near wing have just removed two of the used ammunition boxes, and these are lying on the ground. The four full boxes for the starboard wing guns are on the wooden rack in front of the wing, waiting to be lifted into place. On the right the bowser is already in position, primed to commence refuelling the aircraft. This fighter carries VHF radio, as evidenced by the lack of a tri-angular attachment 'tag' near the top rear of the aerial post, or a wire aerial to the fin (*via Scutts*)

reverting to sending smaller formations of bombers across the Channel, protected by a larger fighter escort. This switch was borne out in No 19 Sqn's kill tally, as after the fierce battle of the 18th, during which the unit claimed five bombers destroyed, the remaining 17 aircraft credited to the squadron in 1940 were all Bf 109Es or Bf 110s.

Flt Sgt George Unwin downed his seventh Bf 109E on 27 September whilst leading Yellow Section on a midday sweep over the Thames Estuary. The squadron intercepted a formation of 50 fighters, which were split into two groups escorting 20 Ju 88As. Following the initial engagement, the combat broke up into a series of dogfights, and Flt Sgt Unwin chased a Bf 109 (probably E-1 Werk-Nr 6162 of 6./JG 52) across Kent and out over the Channel.

In his combat report, he states that 'after about ten minutes aerobatics, he (the Luftwaffe pilot) gave up and flew straight and level. I closed to 50 yards and gave him a seven-second burst. Nothing happened, so I gave him another long burst. Still nothing happened, and so I moved to one side and gave him the remainder of my ammo, in a 30° deflection shot. The aircraft stalled and spun into the sea. Obviously Me 109s are now heavily armoured'.

Unwin saw little action in October, but late in the afternoon of 5 November the Duxford Wing tangled with elements of JGs 26 and 51 for the second time that day – No 19 Sqn had earlier intercepted them along the Kent coast between Dover and Deal. Flt Sgt George Unwin was by this stage flying Spitfire II P7427, which had been delivered to his unit ten days before. In the fading light, a frenetic battle was fought over the Dover cliffs. He claimed a 'He 113' shot down into the sea in flames, the German having moments earlier downed a 'Spitfire', which in reality was probably a No 310 Sqn Hurricane. George's 'Heinkel' was almost certainly Bf 109E-1 Werk-Nr 4868 of 5./JG 51.

The lone No 19 Sqn Spitfire was now well over the Channel, and Flt Sgt Unwin was immediately set upon by more Bf 109s, this time from III./JG 26. Somehow he managed to extricate himself from this hair-raising predicament, although not before P7427 had been so badly shot up that JG 26 Bf 109E ace Hptm Gerhard Schöpfel claimed him as one of two 'kills' accrued on the sortie.

More skirmishes continued as the daylight hours grew shorter, and Flt Sgt George Unwin's penultimate victory was scored ten days after his Channel escape, again in a repaired P7427. Two high-flying recce

Bf 110s of 1(F)./22 were plotted over the Thames Estuary at 1130, and the only units airborne in that area were Nos 19 and 242 Sqns, who had been aloft since 0945 on an abortive convoy patrol. Whilst Bader's Hurricane squadron remained off Harwich looking for the offending ships, 'Sandy' Lane's 12-strong formation was vectored towards the Bf 110s, cruising at around 35,000 ft.

After a long 20-minute chase up the Thames, the Spitfires finally trapped the Bf 110s in a three-section pincer movement after the recce aircraft inexplicably dived eastward from their safe position at altitude. Flt Sgt Unwin, leading Yellow Section of A Flight, fired on one of the rapidly diving Bf 110s at 27,000 ft as it flashed over the top of him. He immediately pointed the nose of his Spitfire seaward, and followed the Messerschmitt down at over 400 mph, intermittently firing. Finally, with the help of 'Yellow Two' – Flg Off Leonard Haines, who scored eight kills and shared four others whilst with No 19 Sqn – the aircraft shed a wing and crashed in the estuary.

On the afternoon of 28 November Flt Sgt Unwin saw action in a Spitfire for the last time. Again the unit were performing a convoy patrol about 30 miles east of Southend when the formation's 'search section' warned the remaining eight pilots of No 19 Sqn that they were about to be bounced by five Bf 109E-4s of I./JG 26. The Messerschmitts went for the rearmost section of Spitfires, but were in turn immediately intercepted by 'Yellow Section', led by George. Flying in line astern formation, the Spitfires chased two of the now fleeing Bf 109s as they raced at ever-decreasing height in a south-easterly direction over the Channel. Despite taking violent evasive action, the *Emils* soon fell within range of the Spitfires' guns, and Flt Sgt Unwin and Sgt David Fulford (4 and 2 shared destroyed) took it in turns to shoot at the rearmost Bf 109 from a range of about 100 yards.

Flying this 1.*Staffel* aircraft (Werk-Nr 3755) from the Pas de Calais was Fw Wolfgang Kaminsky, who soon succumbed to the repeated attacks – his aircraft crashed in a huge spray of water.

As the weather deteriorated during December, and the Luftwaffe restricted their daylight assaults to sporadic 'nuisance' fighter sweeps along the Channel coast, Fighter Command took stock of its assets, both in terms of men and machinery. On 1 December Flt Sgt George Unwin was promoted to Warrant Officer and awarded a bar to his DFM. Soon after this he and fellow pre-war veteran Harry Steere were deemed to be 'too old' for the frontline – George Unwin was three weeks short of his 28th birthday – and duly received postings sending them on a basic instructors' courses within Flying Training Command!

PROFILE OF DESMOND SHEEN

Although the Spitfire Mk I/II fought exclusively on the Channel front, not all of the pilots that attained ace status whilst flying the Supermarine fighter were by any means British. Indeed, of the top ten aces to have flown early-mark Spitfires, three of them were Kiwis, one was a South African and one an Australian. Focusing on the latter nation's contribution in this period, the first Australian to fire his guns in anger during World War 2 was a 22-year-old flying officer by the name of Desmond Frederick Burt Sheen, serving with No 72 Sqn on Spitfires at Leconfield.

Sgt Jennings and X4474 scramble as part of George Unwin's Yellow Section at Fowlmere in September 1940. Like the latter, Jennings was credited with destroying a Bf 109E from JG 54 during the huge dogfight that took place south of the Thames on 27 September – No 19 Sqn pilots claimed eight *Emils* destroyed in this engagement. Sgt Jennings failed to achieve ace status by just a solitary kill, and in spring 1941 was posted to Training Command. He eventually returned to frontline flying in August 1944, joining No 168 Sqn flying firstly Mustang Is and then Typhoon IBs on tactical recce work over France.

X4474 went on to see further frontline service in 1940 with Nos 602 and 610 Sqns, before being relegated to second line training duties. Whilst with the former unit it was used by ace Plt Off Archie Lyall (3 and 3 shared destroyed, 2 probables and 5 and 4 shared damaged) to achieve a probable kill over a Bf 109E of JG 2 on 6 November (*via Scutts*)

A pre-war pilot who had been initially recruited into the Royal Australian Air Force in January 1936, Sheen had learnt his craft on Gladiators upon joining the unit at Church Fenton in July 1937. However, by 1939 the obsolescence of the Gloster fighter was obvious to all those who flew it, and it was therefore with great relief that No 72 Sqn's pilots welcomed their first Spitfires in April 1939, fresh from the Supermarine factory at Woolston, in Southampton.

These Spitfires were part of the very first order (310 aircraft in total) for the Supermarine fighter placed by the RAF, and remained with No 72 Sqn until September 1940. Sheen flew most of these early Mk Is in the months leading up to the declaration of war, and was allowed to adorn K9959 with his personal boomerang emblem.

Unlike many of Fighter Command's pilots, who had to wait until the Wehrmacht's *Blitzkrieg* across Western Europe in May 1940 before they got to encounter the Luftwaffe, Des Sheen claimed his first kill as early as 21 October 1939. With the outbreak of war, No 72 Sqn had moved due east from Church Fenton to its operational station at Leconfield, just north of Hull. This airfield was under the control of No 13 Group who, amongst other things, had the responsibility of protecting the countless coastal convoys that plied the North Sea between the many ports of north-east England. In the early weeks of the 'Phoney War', vessels sailing in this region experienced some of the first tentative attacks staged by the Luftwaffe against British targets, so Fighter Command units on the east coast were given the job of performing a seemingly endless routine of convoy patrols.

No 72 Sqn was perfectly placed for this duty, and on the afternoon of 21 October the unit got lucky. Flg Offs Des Sheen and 'Jimmie' Elsdon (who also later became a Battle of Britain ace with No 72 Sqn, scoring seven kills) were scrambled from readiness and vectored onto a number of contacts some 15 miles south-east of Spurn Head following a report of a convoy under attack by nine Heinkel He 115B floatplanes from 1./*Küstenfliegergruppe* 406.

'We took off as a pair and headed out to sea, where we soon came across the He 115s pressing home their attack. As soon as they spotted us, two of them peeled off and struggled to gained height in order to offer the remaining floatplanes some semblance of top cover. "Jimmie" Elsdon and I immediately took them on, and as I closed on my He 115, its rear gunner attempted to put me off my aim by blazing away with his weapon, but I soon silenced him. The next burst may have then killed the pilot for the Heinkel started to fly very erratically, and with this I turned away to look for another target. I never actually claimed the floatplane as destroyed, but was later credited with it as a confirmed victory.'

Thousands of miles from home, Flg Off Des Sheen of No 72 Sqn left little doubt as to his origins by decorating Spitfire K9959/RN-J with a distinctive brown boomerang on the cockpit hatch. This aircraft was heavily used in the first months of the war by the former Canberra boy (note the weathering of the camouflage on the engine access panel), enjoying a long association with its Australian pilot stretching back to September 1939. He used it to shoot down a He 115 on 21 October 1939 and claim a third of a kill against a He 111 on 7 December that same year, although both the fighter and the pilot were hit during this latter engagement. K9959 finally left No 72 Sqn in mid-August 1940 for a Civilian Repair Unit, where it was converted into a photo-recce platform and subsequently issued to No 1 PRU. It was written off in a forced landing following engine failure at Long Marston, Hertfordshire, on 22 January 1941

Both Elsdon and Sheen had scored single kills over the Heinkels, whilst the Hurricane pilots of No 46 Sqn, stationed at Digby, also claimed three floatplanes destroyed and one damaged (which later crashed in Denmark) from the same formation. This was the last armed recce made by a sizeable force of He 115s into British waters.

Later that same month No 72 Sqn started operating a flight of Spitfires from Drem, near Edinburgh, again on convoy patrols, before moving in squadron-strength to the Scottish airfield in December. Here they shared the station's austere facilities with No 602 'City of Glasgow' Sqn. The former had only been at Drem a matter of days when they encountered the enemy for the second time in less than six weeks. Seven He 111H-3s of 1./KG 26 were picked up on radar heading into the Tay Estuary at midday on 7 December and three patrolling No 603 'City of Edinburgh' Sqn Spitfires from Turnhouse quickly intercepted them. Although the trio inflicted damage on two of the Heinkels, dwindling fuel forced them to break off the attack.

Meanwhile, the alert section of No 72 Sqn back at Drem had been told to scramble as soon as the He 111s had been plotted, and six Spitfires roared across the field and headed out northward over the Firth. Amongst their number was Des Sheen.

'We soon spotted the formation of seven Heinkels, who were carrying out an armed reconnaissance along the east coast. They must have thought that there would be no fighters this far north, so our presence no doubt came as a nasty shock to them. They had dropped down to low level in order to try and evade the No 603 Sqn Spitfires, so we in turn dived down to their altitude – I remember quite vividly zooming past Bell Rock lighthouse at eye-level, in pursuit of a fleeing bomber. As I commenced firing on my chosen target, a gunner in a second He 111 off to the left-hand side of "my" bomber hit me with an accurate burst in the cockpit. I was struck in the ear with one round and hit in the backside with another, whilst a third round ruptured my petrol tank. I immediately broke off my attack and headed south to Leuchars, with my cockpit filling with fuel. Upon landing safely, I was soon bundled into an ambulance and proceeded to spend Christmas convalescing in the hospital in Edinburgh Castle, which was most pleasant!'

Des had been flying K9959 on both sorties in which he had seen action, and after he had landed the damaged fighter at Leuchars on 7 December, the groundcrew assigned to temporarily 'patch up' the fighter prior to it returning to Drem found an incendiary round in the petrol tank that had somehow not ignited when it buried itself in the Spitfire – the Australian had had a fortunate escape. Two Heinkels were downed during this action, with credits being shared between the pilots of Nos 72 and 603 Sqns – Sheen was awarded a third of a kill.

Having spent several weeks in hospital, Des Sheen returned to his unit just in time to bid Scotland farewell and head south back to Church Fenton, via Leconfield. More convoy patrols were then undertaken by the unit, but the enemy was not encountered.

In April Des Sheen left Fighter Command to join a shadowy outfit that went by the name of the Photographic Development Unit (PDU), which was equipped with photo-recce Spitfires. Here he stayed until he requested a transfer back to No 72 Sqn, still based at Acklington, in July. Sheen returned to his old unit as acting flight commander.

Once back, he was reunited with K9959 again, and soon had the boomerang reapplied to the cockpit entry hatch. Over the next six weeks, the pilots at No 72 Sqn watched with envious eyes as their compatriots in No 11 Group were involved in engaging vast armadas of German aircraft hell-bent on destroying the RAF's radar chain and airfields. Many thought that the fight would be over before they would get the chance to test their mettle in combat, but on 15 August, as part of the Luftwaffe's attempt to simultaneously saturate RAF defences across the UK, the Battle of Britain finally came to No 13 Group.

Luftflotte 5 had been tasked with hitting targets along the north-east coast in order to take advantage of what they believed was undefended British soil – Luftwaffe High Command was convinced that virtually all Fighter Command squadrons were committed to repelling attacks in the south-east. They also believed (again wrongly) that the lack of activity in this area would mean that radar plotters would be less vigilant. No less than 72 He 111H-4s from KG 26 set off from Stavanger/Sola, in Norway, bound for selected No 13 Group airfields at 10:00 hours on the morning of the 15th. They were followed from the same airfield by 21 Bf 110Ds from I./ZG 76, led by *Gruppe Kommandeur* Hauptmann Werner Restemeyer, who was flying a specially modified Messerschmitt fitted with radio monitoring equipment in order to listen in on British transmissions. All the *Zerstörer* carried 1000-litre belly tanks (nicknamed *Dachshunds*) which allowed them to cover the vast distance across the North Sea as escorts for the He 111s.

Earlier, a spoof raid of He 115s from 1. and 3./*Küstenfliegergruppe* 506 had crossed the North Sea from Norway to perform a feint attack on Dundee, and thus hopefully draw any defending fighters based around Edinburgh away from the main formation heading for northern England. However, due to a three-degree navigational error perpetrated by the master He 111 crew, the raiders followed an almost identical course to that flown by the floatplanes, and were soon picked up by plotters at the Chain Home Low radar station at Anstruther, on the Fifeshire coast. As planned, the seaplanes turned back some 40 miles from the Scottish coast, but the larger force continued on.

The raid strength was initially judged to be just three aircraft strong, but this was soon amended by the Anstruther plotters to 30+, so the No 13 Group Controller immediately ordered No 72 Sqn to full unit readiness at Acklington at 12:10 hours. The squadron only had to wait five minutes before the order to scramble was relayed to them. Once all 11 Spitfires had taken off, they were told to hold over their base for a short period as the raiders (realising their navigational error) had altered their course and were now heading south down the coast. Des Sheen was leading Green Section, which comprised two pairs of Spitfires. He had been given the responsibility of providing rearguard protection on either flank of the remaining seven No 72 Sqn fighters, and as his unit circled over Acklington, his radio headset came to life with the vectoring co-ordinates that would see the fighters intercept the *Luftflotte* 5 force head on east of the Farne Islands.

Realising just how large the raid was, the Fighter Controller at No 13 Group hastily scrambled two Hurricane squadrons to give No 72 Sqn some assistance. However, these fighters were still struggling to get airborne as Des Sheen's unit sighted the enemy. They had been told to be on the lookout for 30+ bandits, but what lay before them at 18,000 ft was a force of nearly 100 aircraft. The unit was being led on this occasion by future OC, Flt Lt Edward 'Ted' Graham, and he immediately reported to the Controller the raid's strength and composition.

'I had spotted the enemy very early on, and they resembled a large swarm of bees – there was line after line of bombers. Several seconds then passed by, and as "Ted" had failed to report having sighted them, I quickly got on the R/T to him and said "What's wrong? Can't you see the buggers yet?" He replied, "I've seen them all right, but I'm still trying to work out what to do"!', Des Sheen related to series editor Tony Holmes in an interview conducted specially for this volume in February 1996.

Instructing Sheen to remain with his flight above the bombers at 21,000 ft, Graham led Blue and Red Sections down into the enemy formation from the seaward side, thus using the sun to shield their attack. The diving Spitfires were spotted seconds prior to opening fire on the bombers, and the Bf 110 pilots quickly jettisoned their *Dachshunds* in order to intercept the British fighters. As the Messerschmitts formed up into their infamous defensive circles – known as the *Abwehrkreis* – and the He 111s broke into two main

Spitfire I of No 72 Sqn seen in June 1940 with the fin stripe introduced the previous month. Note the 'blinker' fitted on the fuselage just in front of the cockpit – a squadron-level modification bolted onto the fighter to shield the pilot's eyes from the glare of the exhaust stubs during night flying. Like Sheen's K9959, this aircraft also has a personal marking painted in a white shield beneath the 'blinker' (*via Sheen*)

groups (one heading north towards Clyde and the other south to Newcastle), Sheen ordered Green Section into the meleé.

'I latched onto a formation of seven Bf 110s that had begun attempting to turn in a circle, and I quickly singled out their leader. I initially identified this machine as a Ju 88, simply because I was mesmerised by what I thought was a bloody great bomb affixed to the aircraft's centreline. I took aim and fired at very close range and the Messerschmitt simply blew up in front of me. This was very alarming, as I had to fly straight through the smoke and debris left behind by the now disintegrated fighter, but fortunately I emerged unscathed.'

His victim was Hauptmann Restemeyer, and although it was initially thought that the pilot had been unable to jettison his empty belly tank, it is now widely believed that the *Gruppen Kommandeur* was actually flying a rare Bf 110D-0 variant, which featured a fixed nose-mounted ventral tank. In either case, the now-vacuous fuel cell was full of highly explosive fumes, and several carefully aimed rounds of .303-in ammunition from Sheen's K9959 was all that was needed to trigger a devastating mid-air explosion. Having despatched one Bf 110, the Australian pilot had begun to gain altitude when he spotted another formation of six *Zerstörer* heading back out to sea.

'As I climbed to attack them one of the Messerschmitts broke away and dived down straight at me, its four machine-gun and twin cannon nose armament firing intermittently. I instinctively fired back, the Bf 110 looming ever larger in my sights. Fortunately, I was a better shot than my opponent and his port engine caught fire. However, we were still on a collision course, and I was forced to "bunt" my Spitfire under the Messerschmitt to avoid hitting him. That was the last I saw of my foe, the stricken fighter leaving a trail of thickening smoke as it dived earthward. I turned to find another target, but just as the sky had been full of targets one minute, I now found myself alone, so I returned to Acklington – the combat had lasted just five minutes.'

It is likely that the second Bf 110D tackled by Des Sheen was the Stab I./ZG 76 machine flown by *Gruppe* Adjutant Oberleutnant Loobes, the fighter crashing into the sea. Although flushed with success, the pilots at Acklington knew that things would be much tougher down south, and braced themselves for the inevitable posting to No 11 Group. Two weeks later the signal they had all been waiting for arrived – No 72 Sqn was to move to Biggin Hill on 31 August in a straight swap with the remnants of No 610 'County of Chester' Sqn.

Following one last unhurried breakfast on a warm and sunny Saturday morning, No 72 Sqn bade farewell to their Northumberland home and headed south into the maelstrom of 'Hellfire Corner'. What greeted the unit upon its arrival at its new station was a scene of total devastation. Biggin Hill had been badly bomb just the day before, and as if to finish off the job once and for all, the Luftwaffe hit it again at noon on the 31st. Somehow, all 15 Spitfires managed to land between the hurriedly filled in craters, and dispersed on the edge of the airfield. Yet another sizeable raid had already been detected coming in across the Channel, and as soon as the unit's Spitfires had been refuelled, No 72 Sqn took off late in the afternoon to intercept the enemy.

One Spitfire was left behind, its Merlin engine refusing to start once it had been refuelled – sat in the cockpit watching his comrades disappear over the horizon was Des Sheen. Having at last coaxed the fighter into life, he charged away from the dispersal with the Merlin's engine note rapidly increasing as he roared across the airfield and took off alone, vainly trying to catch up with the remainder of the unit.

Once airborne, No 72 Sqn was vectored onto a formation of Do 17Z-2s of I./KG 3 over Dungeness, but had been bounced by the bombers' Bf 109E escort prior to interception. Two Spitfires were lost to the *Emils*, with one pilot being killed and the second baling out badly wounded. A single Dornier latter crashed near St Omer due to damage inflicted by the unit on its only pass at the bombers.

Sheen never managed to make contact with his squadron prior to them engaging the enemy, and after completing a lone patrol over Kent, landed back at Biggin Hill to find that both the remnants of his unit had returned and that the airfield had been bombed yet again.

'After I had landed and taxied to the dispersal, having safely negotiated more fresh bomb craters that littered my path, a WAAF driver collected me and drove me back to my makeshift billet, skirting around unexploded bombs as she went. Biggin was virtually inoperable, and at dawn the next morning the squadron flew out to Croydon Airport, where facilities were somewhat better. At mid-morning we were ordered off to intercept a force of roughly 30 Do 17Zs, escorted by an equal number of Bf 109Es, that was heading for the London Docks. It was a beautifully sunny Sunday morning, and we quickly spotted the enemy formation. Manoeuvring into position for a stern attack on the Dorniers, I switched on the gunsight and took the safety catch off the gun button. I had a bomber squared up in my sights and had just started to open fire when all hell broke loose around me. My Spitfire lurched and the cockpit began to fill with smoke, so I broke off my abortive attack and dropped away from the bomber formation. I had not seen my attacker, but later found out that we had been bounced out of the sun by six Bf 109Es flying top cover.

'I tried to level out but the engine had been struck by cannon shells, and when I saw flames starting to appear through the smoke I realised that it was time to bale out. I pulled the canopy back, unpinned my straps, rolled the fighter onto its back and fell out of the stricken Spitfire. I was quite high up at 12,000 ft when my parachute opened, and during the several minutes it took me to reach the ground I had a grandstand view of much of the morning's battle over Kent. Bombs were going off in the London Docks area and jettisoned ordnance was falling near Dover. AA batteries were firing all around me, and there was a scrap going on above me, thus filling the sky with noise.

'Several dogfights were also going on, and a Bf 109 went down quite close by in flames – I think it was the pilot of this aircraft that baled out not too far away from me. His parachute opened up safely, but his harness must have been faulty for he fell out of it and plunged to his death. When I finally touched down in a field, a young girl ran over and shyly watched me start to gather up my parachute.'

Two other Spitfires had fallen to the Bf 109s during this unseen attack, with one pilot being killed, whilst a further two had force landed at West Malling, having suffered severely at the hands of the *Emils*.

In April 1940 Des Sheen was 'chosen' to join a recently formed Spitfire outfit known as the Photographic Development Unit (PDU) following the arrival of a signal at No 72 Sqn's Acklington base asking for volunteers. His OC, Sqn Ldr Ronald Lees (a pre-war Australian permanent commission officer who had commanded the unit since December 1938), hit on the novel idea of putting all the names of the unit's pilots into a hat and choosing one at random. Sheen's was duly drawn out, and for the next four months he flew photo-reconnaissance missions in specially converted (and unarmed) Spitfire PR Mk Is like this one from both Britain and France with No 212 Sqn – his award of the DFC was gazetted whilst he was attached to the PDU (*via Sheen*)

Later that afternoon two more Spitfires returned to Croydon badly shot up following a dogfight with Bf 109s over Dungeness.

Having recovered from being shot down on the 1st, and been officially promoted to the rank of flight lieutenant on the 3rd, Des Sheen saw combat again on the afternoon of 4 September when his squadron was one of nine to intercept a 300-aircraft strong attack over south-east Kent. Running into two formations of 'freelancing' Bf 110s from II./ZG 76 over Tenterden, the No 72 Sqn pilots engaged the enemy just as they began manoeuvring into their now familiar defensive circles. Wary of been shot down by an unseen enemy from above, Sheen checked the sky behind him before picking out a Bf 110 that was just about to enter an *Abwehrkreis*. Taking aim, he opened up with a long burst, which knocked out the fighter's port engine, but he had allowed his closing speed to build up too much in the dive to interception and was forced to break away to avoid colliding with the *Zerstörer*.

Climbing back up to 20,000 ft, Sheen looked around for another target, but the sky was now empty, so he returned by himself to Croydon. Once back at base he lodged a claim for a probable kill, which in reality should have been upgraded to a confirmed victory for his quarry (Bf 110C Werk-Nr 3287) had ditched in the Channel seven miles off Pevensey Bay – a pilot from No 234 Sqn was also credited with a share of this kill. No 72 Sqn pilots claimed a further two ZG 76 Bf 110s destroyed, but in return had two Spitfires shot down and a third badly damaged by cannon fire sustained during a head-on pass with a *Zerstörer* – all three pilots escaped injury.

Although No 72 Sqn hadn't lost a pilot in action in three days of bitter fighting, it had seen no less than 11 Spitfires written off and more than half a dozen badly damaged. Therefore, when the unit was scrambled in mid-afternoon from Hawkinge to intercept bombers heading for Thameshaven, only nine aircraft were declared serviceable to take part in the sortie. One of these was X4034, flown on this occasion by Des Sheen, who was leading the squadron in place of the wounded Sqn Ldr Anthony Collins. Like most other squadrons in Fighter Command, the unit was still using the rigid pre-war tactic of engaging the enemy in 'battle formation', which comprised three or four tight vics (covered by two 'weavers' at the rear protecting the leader). Struggling to gain height over Canterbury, No 72 Sqn paid the price for adhering to this now antiquated tactic.

Only spotted when it was too late by the 'weavers', a *Schwarm* of Bf 109Es attacked out of the sun and quickly inflicted mortal damage on the rear three Spitfires. Before the unit could react to this vicious attack, their assailants had disappeared, leaving two pilots to crash to their death, and the third, Flt Lt Des Sheen, fighting to extricate himself from his now virtually wingless Spitfire.

'One of our "weavers" shouted out a warning that he had sighted enemy fighters above us, but just as his voice crackled over the R/T my aircraft shuddered as it was hit by cannon and machine-gun rounds. I was hit in several places by shell splinters, and my oxygen bottle was punctured, which caused me to pass out. When I finally came to, my aircraft was in an uncontrollable vertical dive, so I forced the canopy back and released the harness pins in preparation for baling out. However, as soon as the straps came free I was sucked out my seat, but then I was snagged by my feet on the windscreen, which laid me out in the slipstream of the aircraft along its spine. The Spitfire was rapidly nearing the ground, but fortunately I was thrown clear and immediately pulled the ripcord. My parachute opened at just 800 ft, and my landing was broken by a copse of trees – so much so, that my only real injuries were those sustained in the attack itself. The first person on the scene was a policeman on a bicycle who, whilst offering me a drink from his hip flask, asked "You left it a bit late didn't you?"!'

Sheen was taken to Queen Mary's Hospital in Sidcup, and following a spell of sick leave, returned to Biggin Hill on 13 October – just in time to head back to Leconfield with his unit, which had been replaced at Biggin by No 74 Sqn. No 72 Sqn had been reduced to just seven pilots, having lost nine killed and seen 24 Spitfires written off in six weeks of near-constant fighting over south-east England.

Over the winter of 1941 the unit returned to full strength and was tasked once again with protecting coastal convoys. When the Luftwaffe's bombing tactic switched to the night blitz, more and more raiders started entering No 13 Group's airspace, hitting targets around Newcastle, Edinburgh and Glasgow. Fighter Command was then virtually powerless to stop bombers at night, although Spitfire and Hurricane units would often be tasked with performing much-disliked patrols in aircraft that were far from suitable for nightfighting. No 72 Sqn was still flying Spitfires Is at this point, and Des Sheen's last kill came during a night patrol on 13/14 March – Ju 88A-5 Werk-Nr 2234 of 3./*Küstenfliegergruppe* 106, which was on a raid to Glasgow.

Recently promoted Flt Lt Des Sheen is seen just after his release from Queen Mary's Hospital in Sidcup in early October 1940 (*via Sheen*)

He had spent many fruitless hours in the cockpit of a Spitfire at night during the winter of 1941, fighting the cold and poor weather whilst searching for a stealthy enemy, but on this occasion luck was with him, being vectored onto a contact during a period of moonlight.

'The bomber was exactly where the Controller indicated it would be, and I opened up with a long burst, which lit the enemy aircraft up like a "Catherine Wheel" and started a fire in one of its engines. I pressed home my attack to the point where I almost rammed the bomber, my windscreen becoming smeared with oil from the stricken aircraft. I didn't hang around to see it crash, but I later learnt that it had indeed been spotted by naval observers plunging into the sea.'

The following month Sheen was promoted to squadron leader and given command of No 72 Sqn, which re-equipped with Mk IIAs (plus several cannon-armed IIBs) and headed south to No 11 Group at Biggin Hill once again. Fighter Command's new campaign of attrition against the *Jagdwaffe* through its wing offensive was now getting into full swing, and the Des Sheen/No 72 Sqn partnership forged over four years of war and peace was to be in its vanguard.

THE APPENDICES

Specifications

First Production Spitfire I K9787, Tested August 1938

Type: single-seat interceptor fighter
Armament: eight .303-in machine guns with 300 rounds per gun
Powerplant: one Rolls-Royce Merlin II engine rated at 900 bhp for take-off, 1060 bhp at 17,000 ft
Dimensions: span 36 ft 10 in, length 29 ft 11 in, height 12 ft 3 in (over airscrew disc), wing area 242 sq ft
Weights: max loaded 5819 lbs, empty 4482 lbs.
Performance: maximum speed 362 mph at 18,500 ft, climb to 20,000 ft in 9 mins 25 secs, service ceiling 31,900 ft
Notes: this aircraft was fitted with a carved wooden two-bladed propeller, and flat-topped canopy. It carried no armour or other protection for the pilot

Mid-Run Production Spitfire I N3171, Tested March 1940

(Note: details given only where they differ from those for the aircraft above)
Powerplant: one Rolls-Royce Merlin III engine rated at 900 bhp for take-off, 1060 bhp at 17,000 ft
Weights: max loaded 6050 lbs, empty 4713 lbs
Performance: maximum speed 353 mph at 20,000 ft, climb to 20,000 ft in 7 min 42 secs, service ceiling 34,700 ft
Notes: this aircraft was fitted with a Rotol three-bladed constant speed propeller, and domed canopy. It carried a toughened glass slab in front of the windscreen but no armour behind the pilot

First Production Spitfire II P7280, tested September 1940

(Note: details given only where they differ from those for the aircraft above)
Powerplant: one Rolls-Royce Merlin XII engine, maximum power 1140 bhp at 14,750 ft at +9 lbs boost (emergency power setting, five minutes maximum) using 100 octane fuel
Weights: max loaded 6172 lbs, empty 4783 lbs
Performance: maximum speed 354 mph at 17,554 ft, climb to 20,000 ft in 7 mins, service ceiling 37,600 ft
Notes: this aircraft was fitted with a Rotol three-bladed constant speed propeller, a domed canopy and IFF equipment. It carried a toughened glass slab in front of the windscreen and also 73 lbs of steel armour plate behind the pilot

Production Spitfire II (Long Range) P8036, tested September 1941

(Note: details given only where they differ from those for the aircraft above)
Powerplant: one Rolls-Royce Merlin XII engine, maximum power 1140 bhp at 14,750 ft at +9 lbs boost (emergency power setting, five minutes maximum) using 100 octane fuel
Weights: max loaded 6513 lbs, empty 4836 lbs
Performance: maximum speed 328 mph at 16,500 ft, climb to 20,000 ft in 9 mins 48 secs, service ceiling 33,900 ft
Notes: this aircraft carried an additional 40 gallon fuel tank fixed in position under the port wing, bringing its total fuel load to 125 gallons

Spitfire Mk I versus Bf 109E

On 22 November 1939 the French Air Force was presented with a virtually intact Bf 109E-3 (1/JG 76's 'White 14', Werk-Nr 1304) when it force-landed at Woerth, in the Bas-Rhin Department. After protracted flight trials in France, the aircraft was lent to the Royal Aircraft Establishment at Farnborough in May 1940 for further testing. During one of these trials, a Spitfire fitted with the new Rotol constant-speed propeller was flown in mock combat against the German fighter. In July 1940, as the Battle of Britain was in its opening phase, the following report appeared;

'*Comparative Trial between Me 109 and "Rotol" Spitfire*

1. The trial commenced with the two aircraft taking off together, with the Spitfire slightly behind and using +6 lbs boost and 3000 rpm.

2. When fully airborne, the pilot of the Spitfire reduced his engine revolutions to 2650 rpm and was then able to overtake and outclimb the Me 109. At 4000 ft, the Spitfire pilot was 1000 ft above the Me 109, from which position he was able to get on to its tail, and remain there within effective range despite all efforts of the pilot of the Me 109 to shake him off.

3. The Spitfire then allowed the Me 109 to get on to his tail and attempted to shake him off. This was found quite easy owing to the superior manoeuvrability of his aircraft, particularly in the looping plane and at low speeds between 100 and 140 mph. By executing a steep turn just above stalling speed, he ultimately got back into a position on the tail of the Me 109.

4. Another effective form of evasion with the Spitfire was found to be a steep, climbing spiral at 120 mph, using +6 lbs boost and 2650 rpm; in this manoeuvre, the Spitfire gained rapidly on the Me 109, eventually allowing the pilot to execute a half roll, on to the tail of his opponent.

5. Comparative speed trials were then carried out, and the Spitfire proved to be considerably the faster of the two, both in acceleration and straight and level flight, without

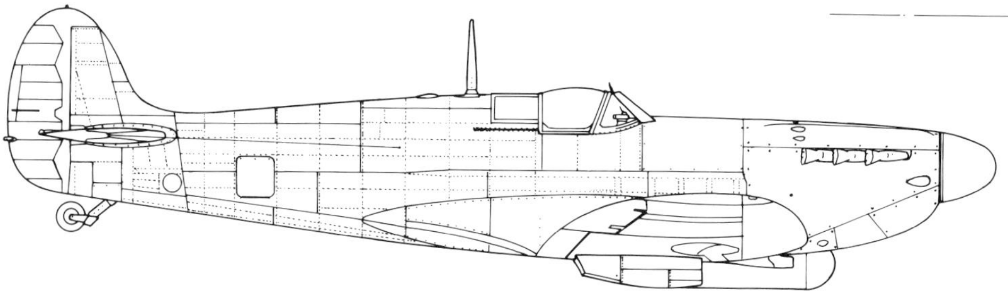

All drawings on this page are of a Spitfire Mk IIA Long Range, 1/72nd scale

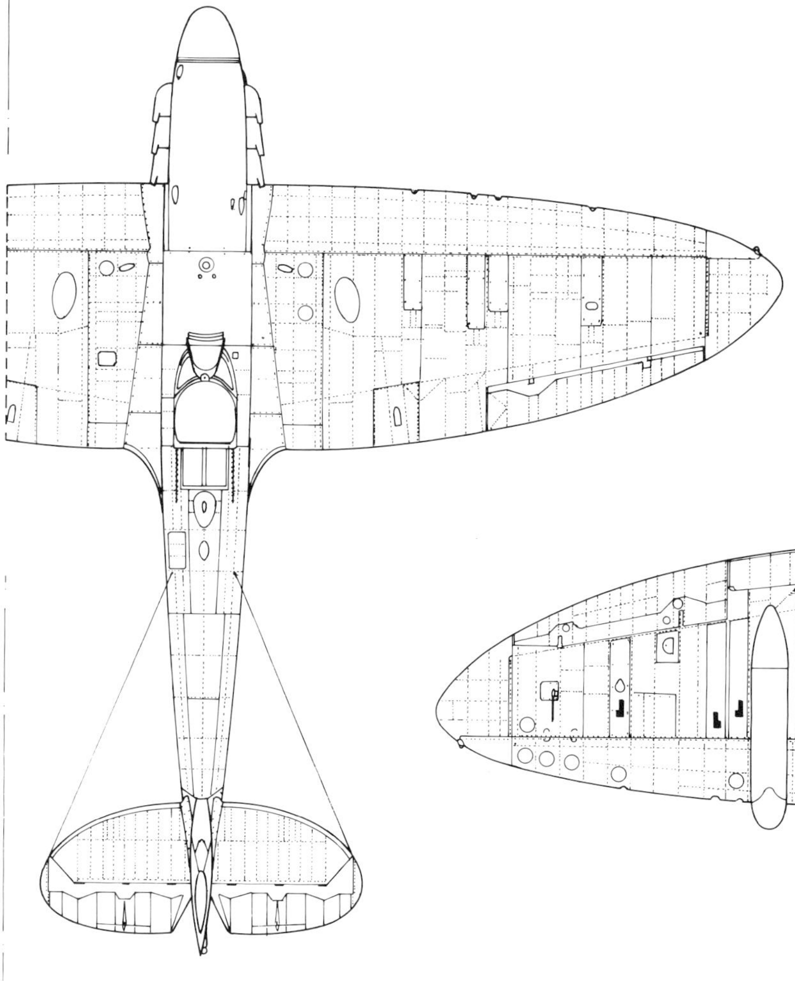

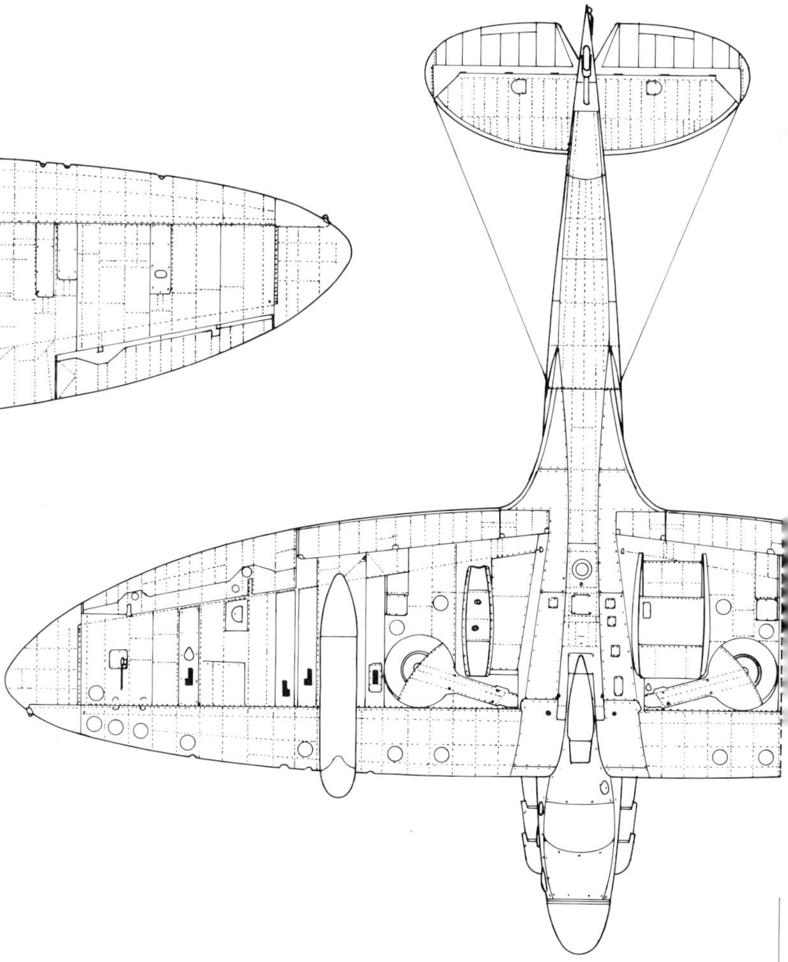

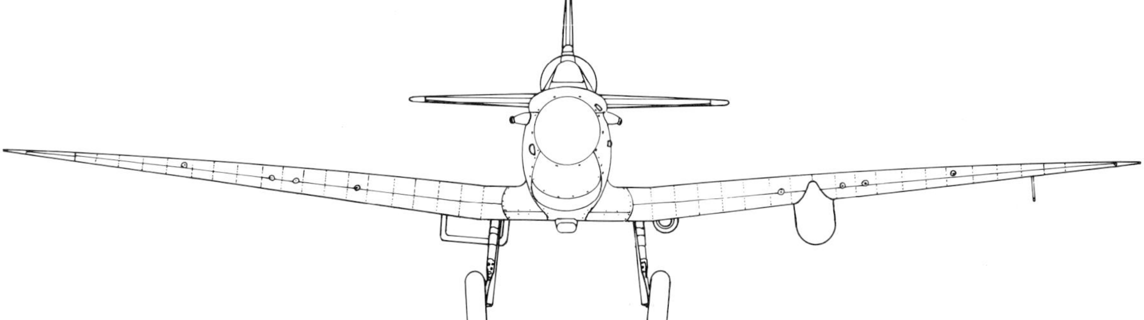

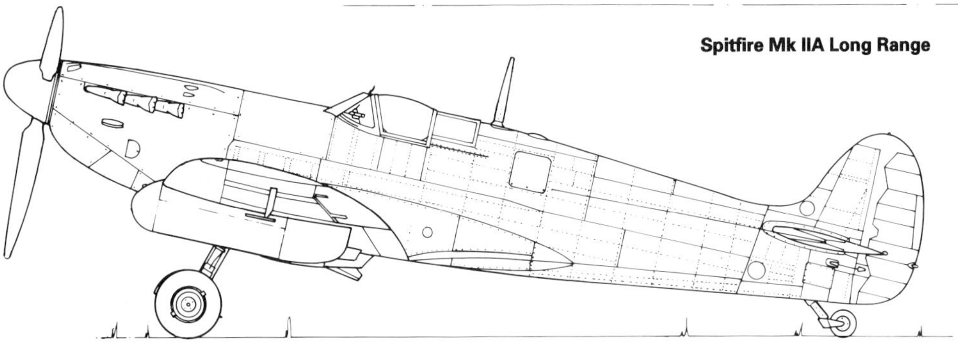

Spitfire Mk IIA Long Range

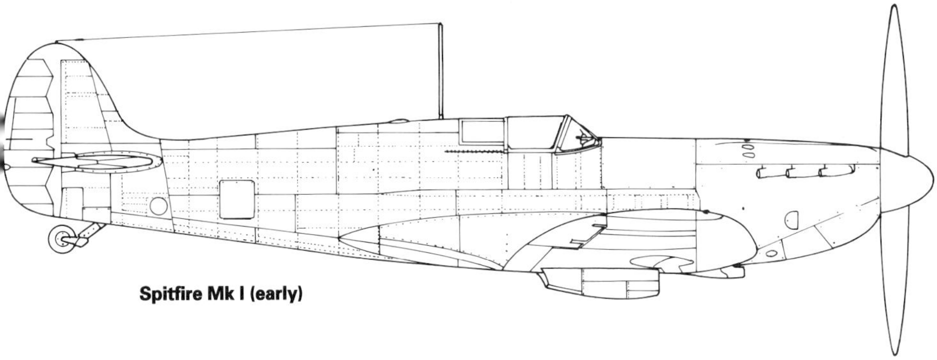

Spitfire Mk I (early)

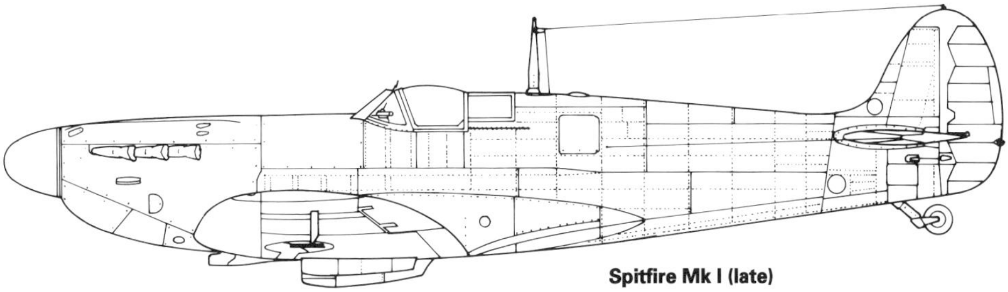

Spitfire Mk I (late)

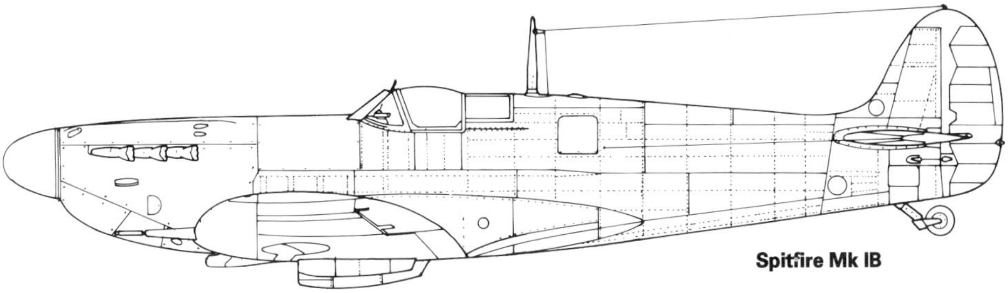

Spitfire Mk IB

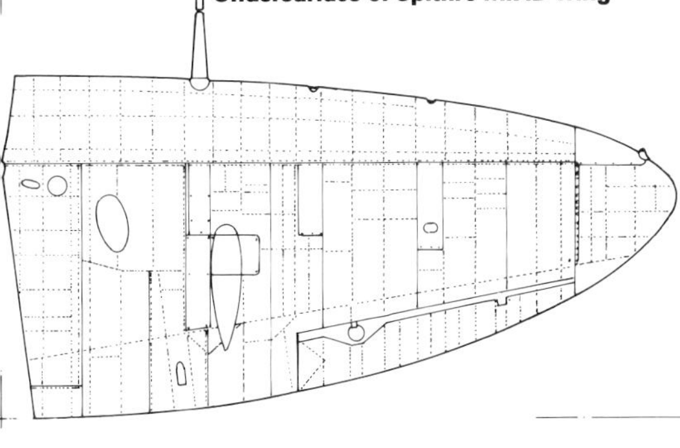

Undersurface of Spitfire Mk IB wing

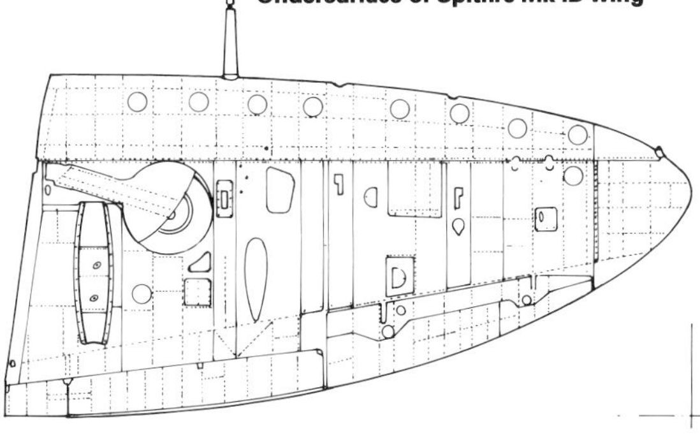

Undersurface of Spitfire Mk IB wing

having to make use of the emergency +12 lbs boost. During diving trials, the Spitfire pilot found that, by engaging fully coarse pitch and using -2 lbs boost, his aircraft was superior to the Me 109.'

The trial 'proved' that the Spitfire was considerably superior to its Luftwaffe counterpart on almost all counts. The fundamental flaw in these findings was that few German fighter pilots would allow themselves to get into a low speed, low altitude, turning fight with a Spitfire, and few of those that did would live to tell the tale. Their tactics when engaging Spitfires were similar to those used against the yet more manoeuvrable Russian-built fighters over Spain. The Messerschmitts cruised over the battle area at high altitude until they sighted their opponents. They then manoeuvred into a favourable position above their prey, and launched high speed diving attacks on their victims. After each such attack the fighters zoomed back to a position of safety at high altitude, and their pilots re-assessed the situation. The Spitfire's superior low altitude manoeuvrability was of little value against such tactics.

Interestingly, the Luftwaffe test centre at Rechlin also carried out comparative fighting trials between Bf 109s and a captured Spitfire I. In this case, however, the British fighter was fitted with a two-pitch airscrew. The conclusions drawn from the tests there were quite different from those drawn from the trials in Great Britain. One of those who flew the Spitfire (and also a captured Hurricane) was fighter ace Hauptmann Werner Mölders. Later he wrote

'It was very interesting to carry out the flight trials at Rechlin with the Spitfire and the Hurricane. Both types are very simple to fly compared with our aircraft, and childishly easy to take-off and land (compared with the Bf 109). The Hurricane is very good-natured and turns well, but its performance is decidedly inferior to that of the Bf 109. It has strong stick forces and is "lazy" on the ailerons. The Spitfire is one class better. It handles well, is light on the controls, faultless in the turn and has a performance approaching that of the Bf 109. As a fighting aircraft, however, it is miserable. A sudden push forward on the stick will cause the motor to cut. Also, because the propeller has only two pitch settings (take-off and cruise), in a rapidly changing air combat situation the motor is either overspeeding or else it is not being used to the full.'

The two sets of trials showed that the 'home team' possessed the superior fighter type. Given the naivety with which the trials were conducted, any other finding would probably have been regarded as 'politically incorrect'. War provided the acid test of the two fighters' capabilities vis-a-vis each other. In the Battle of Britain most fighter-versus-fighter combats took place in the height band between 13,000 and 20,000 ft, because that was where the German bombers flew. At that altitude the Mark I and Mark II Spitfires were roughly equal to the Bf 109 in capability. In the fleeting air combats that were the norm, tactical initiative counted for far more than the relatively small performance differences that existed between the opposing fighter types.

RAF FIGHTER COMMAND SPITFIRE UNITS 14 SEPTEMBER 1940

Given below is the Fighter Command order of battle of units equipped with Mark I and II Spitfires on the evening of 14 September 1940, those held in reserve at maintenance units ready for issue and those with operational training units. Also given is the number of Spitfire delivered to the service during the preceding week. On the following day, the 15th, the Command would fight the action that decided the Battle.

(First figure aircraft serviceable, in brackets aircraft unserviceable)

No 10 Group, HQ Box, Wiltshire

Middle Wallop Sector		
No 609 Sqn	15	(3) Middle Wallop
No 152 Sqn	17	(2) Warmwell
St Eval Sector		
No 234 Sqn	16	(1) St Eval
Group Total	**48**	**(6)**

No 11 Group, HQ Uxbridge, Middlesex

Biggin Hill Sector		
No 72 Sqn	10	(7) Biggin Hill
No 92 Sqn	16	(1) Biggin Hill
No 66 Sqn	14	(2) Gravesend
Hornchurch Sector		
No 603 Sqn	14	(5) Hornchurch
No 41 Sqn	12	(6) Rochford
No 222 Sqn	11	(3) Rochford
Tangmere Sector		
No 602 Sqn	15	(4) Westhampnett
Group Total	**92**	**(28)**

No 12 Group, HQ Watnall, Nottinghamshire

Duxford Sector		
No 19 Sqn	14	(0) Fowlmere
Coltishall Sector		
No 74 Sqn	14	(8) Coltishall
Wittering Sector		
No 266 Sqn	14	(5) Wittering
Digby Sector		
No 611 Sqn	17	(1) Digby
Kirton-in-Lindsey Sector		
No 616 Sqn	14	(4) Kirton-in-Lindsey
No 64 Sqn	7	(3) Leconfield
	6	(3) Ringway
Group Total	**86**	**(24)**

No 13 Group, HQ Newcastle, Northumberland

Catterick Sector		
No 54 Sqn	15	(2) Catterick
Usworth Sector		
No 610 Sqn	14	(5) Acklington
Turnhouse Sector		
No 65 Sqn	15	(5) Turnhouse
Group Total	**44**	**(12)**

Spitfires held at Maintenance Units

Ready for Immediate Issue	47
Ready for Issue in Four Days	10

Spitfires held by Operational Training Units	26 (24)
Spitfire production in the week prior to 14 September	38

COLOUR PLATES

1

Mk IIA P7966/D-B of Wg Cdr Douglas Bader, OC Tangmere Wing, March 1941

This aircraft was one of the first to carry the Wing Leader's initials on the fuselage – it was also a presentation Spitfire, wearing the legend *Manxman* below the cockpit on its starboard side. At the time Bader was taken prisoner in August 1941 his victory score stood at 20 and 4 shared destroyed, 6 and 1 shared probably destroyed and 11 damaged. Issued initially to No 616 Sqn (part of Bader's Wing), this aircraft later served with Nos 412 and 154 Sqns. It was then spent time with Nos 61 and 52 OTUs in 1942, before crashing the following October whilst serving with the latter unit.

2

Mk I K9854/QV-W of Flt Lt Wilfred Clouston, No 19 Sqn, Duxford, October 1939

K9854 was damaged in a mid-air collision and the subsequent crash landing in October 1939, being reduced to components following the accident. Clouston went on to fight in the Battle of Britain, and his score reached 9 and 3 shared destroyed, one and one shared probably destroyed and one shared damaged. In 1941 he was posted to Singapore to command a fighter squadron, but was taken prisoner when the fortress fell and spent the rest of the war in captivity.

3

Mk IB R6776/QV-H of Flt Sgt George Unwin, No 19 Sqn, Fowlmere, August 1940

This aircraft was one of the original cannon-armed Spitfire IBs issued to No 19 Sqn for a brief period in the summer of 1940. Unlike the majority of the unit's pilots, who struggled with the reliability of the twin cannon armament in their Mk IBs, Unwin enjoyed some success in this aircraft, claiming a Bf 110 destroyed and another probably destroyed on 16 August, followed by a third Bf 110 confirmed on 3 September. Later modified into a Mk VB, it went on to serve with Nos 92, 316 and 306 Sqns, before being written off in May 1942 after sustaining Category E battle damage on a sweep over France.

4

Mk I P9386/QV-K of Sqn Ldr Brian Lane, OC No 19 Sqn, Fowlmere, September 1940

Lane was flying this aircraft on 7 September when he shot down a Bf 110 of Stab II./ZG 2 near North Weald – it was also used by No 19 Sqn ace Flt Lt Walter Lawson to down a Bf 110 two days later, and a He 111 on 11 September. After a brief period with No 152 Sqn, the Spitfire went to No 58 OTU in 1941, and continued to perform second line tasks until it was written off in May 1944 whilst serving with No 57 OTU. As this profile shows, P9386 stood out from other Battle of Britain period Spitfires thanks to its non-standard yellow prop spinner – reputedly a hangover from its brief OTU service.

5

Mk IIA P7849/QV-J *Armagh of* Flt Lt Walter Lawson, No 19 Sqn, Fowlmere, June 1941

Lawson used this aircraft on 27 June to shoot down a Bf

109E confirmed and claim a second *Emil* as a probable near St Omer – No 19 Sqn's first kills in seven months. Later, the Spitfire was converted into a Mk V, and in November 1942 transferred to the USAAF. Walter 'Farmer' Lawson claimed 6 and 1 shared destroyed, 3 probables and 1 damaged during his 16 months with No 19 Sqn. Given command of the unit in July 1941 following Sqn Ldr Lane's departure, Lawson was posted missing on a sortie to Rotterdam on 28 August.

6

Mk IIA P7666/EB-Z *OBSERVER CORPS* of Sqn Ldr Donald Finlay, OC No 41 Sqn, Hornchurch, November 1940

Finlay was flying this aircraft on 23 November when he was credited with the destruction of a Bf 109E near Tonbridge – he got a second *Emil* over the same area in P7666 four days later. Don Finlay finished the war with 4 and 2 shared destroyed and 3 and 1 damaged, all on Spitfires. P7666 later served with No 54 Sqn, and was shot down by a Bf 109 whilst being flown by Spitfire ace Plt Off Jack Stokoe (7 and 1 shared destroyed, 2 and 1 shared probable, 4 damaged) on 20 April 1941 – he had just downed a Bf 110 prior to falling victim to the JG 51 machine.

7

Mk I N3173/KL-N of Plt Off Colin Gray, No 54 Sqn, Hornchurch, May 1940

Gray was flying this aircraft over Dunkirk on 25 May 1940 (as described in the text) when he claimed a Bf 109E probably destroyed, but was himself nearly shot down. He brought the Spitfire back to Hornchurch with severe battle damage, and after being repaired it was issued to No 152 Sqn at Warmwell, in Dorset. On 20 September it was being flown by Australian Sgt K C Holland who, after mortally damaging a He 111P of 6./KG 55, made the fatal mistake of closing in on his quarry to check on his aim and was shot down and killed.

8

Mk I N3183/KL-B *KIWI* of Plt Off Alan Deere, No 54 Sqn, Hornchurch, May 1940

Deere used this aircraft to shoot down a Bf 109E (24 May) and a Bf 110 (25 May) during actions in support of the Dunkirk evacuation, where he was credited with seven victories (plus 1 shared, 1 unconfirmed and 1 damaged) in just five days. The aircraft was shot down by elements of II./JG 51 in a bitter action over the Channel on 9 July 1940, its pilot, Plt Off A Evershed, being killed – No 54 Sqn lost two other Spitfires in this action, with a second pilot being killed and Al Deere being slightly burnt when he had to force land P9398 near Manston.

9

Mk I P9389/KL-A of Sqn Ldr James Leathart, OC No 54 Sqn, Hornchurch, May 1940

'Prof' Leathart was flying this aircraft on 21 May when he engaged a He 111 near Dunkirk during one of the first engagements by Spitfires over northern France – he was awarded an unconfirmed kill for the Heinkel. Leathart led No 54 Sqn throughout the summer of 1940, and eventually finished the war with a tally of 7 and 1 shared destroyed, 3 and 1 shared unconfirmed, 2 probables and 3 damaged – all bar one of his kills was scored flying Spitfire Mk Is. P9389 was shot down by a Bf 109 during the afternoon of 24 August 1940, its pilot, Kiwi Plt Off C Stewart, baling out at 20,000 ft and landing safely in the Thames Estuary.

10

Mk I P9554/K-SH of Plt Off James O'Meara, No 64 Sqn, Kenley, August 1940

While flying this aircraft between 12/15 August 1940, O'Meara was credited with three enemy aircraft destroyed (two Bf 109Es and a Ju 88) and three (He 111s) damaged – he finished the war with 11 and 2 shared destroyed, 1 unconfirmed destroyed, 4 probables and 11 and 1 shared damaged. On 16 August the aircraft was flown by No 64 Sqn OC, Sqn Ldr Donald MacDonnell (9 and 1 shared destroyed, 3 unconfirmed destroyed, 1 probable and 7 damaged), who claimed one Bf 109E destroyed, a second as a probable and a third *Emil* damaged, a half share in a He 111 destroyed and a second Heinkel damaged during action over Kent. Heading back to Hawkinge, his ammunition exhausted, MacDonnell was jumped by a Bf 109 and forced to bale out of P9554.

11

Mk I K9906/FZ-L of Flt Lt Robert Stanford Tuck, No 65 Sqn, Hornchurch, August 1939

This aircraft later served with No 64 Sqn during the Battle of Britain before being retired to second line duties with No 7 OTU. It was one of a number of Mk Is converted into PR IIIs for the photo recce role and issued to No 1 PRU at RAF Benson. Tuck was the first Spitfire ace, scoring his fourth and fifth kills (both Do 17s) over Dunkirk on 24 May 1940.

12

Mk I N3035/LZ-X of Plt Off Hubert Allen, No 66 Sqn, Kenley, September 1940

'Dizzy' Allen (5 and 3 shared destroyed, 2 and 1 shared probable and 3 and 1 shared damaged) flew this machine on numerous occasions during the summer of 1940, the Spitfire having been delivered to the unit at Duxford in September 1939. It suffered serious damage in a dogfight over Kent on 29 September whilst being flown by Sgt Peter Willcocks, taking ten months to repair. Ironically, the latter lost his life when his Spitfire collided with a similar machine flown by Plt Off Allen during a patrol over Kent on 28 November 1940.

13

Mk I X4321/LZ-F of Plt Off Crelin 'Bogle' Bodie, No 66 Sqn, Kenley, September 1940

'Bogle' Bodie (5 and 5 shared destroyed, 1 unconfirmed destroyed, 8 and 2 shared probables, 3 and 1 damaged) made a forced landing in this aircraft on 7 September near Hawkinge following combat with Bf 109s off Dover – It had only flown for the first time just nine days before. Although initially struck off charge as having been too badly damaged, X4321 was sent to Heston Aircraft Limited where repairs were effected. By December 1940 the fighter had been restored to its former glory, and went on to serve with Nos 64 and 303 Sqns, before being issued No 58 OTU. It ended its days with this unit in a flying accident in 1942.

14

Mk IIA P7308/XR-D of Plt Off William Dunn, No 71 'Eagle' Sqn, North Weald, August 1941

On 27 August Dunn was flying this aircraft (as part of 100-strong Spitfire escort force for nine Blenheims attacking the steelworks at Lille) when he claimed two Bf 109Fs destroyed (out of an attacking force of 30), making him the first 'Eagle' squadron pilot to achieve five victories – three on Hurricane IIs – and therefore the first American ace of the war. During the same engagement his own aircraft was hit, losing its right wingtip and having its rudder shot up, whilst Dunn suffered wounds to his foot and right leg – after months in hospital, he went on to fly with the USAAF's 406th FG on P-47Ds, raising his score to 9 destroyed, 3 unconfirmed destroyed and 1 and 1 shared probable. P7308 had served with Nos 74, 54 and 308 Sqns prior to being issued to the Americans in August 1941. It was converted into a Mk VA whilst being repaired, and later served with Nos 133, 421, 164 and 602 Sqns, before ending its days with No 61 OTU in July 1943.

15

Mk I (serial unknown)/RN-J of Flt Lt Desmond Sheen, No 72 Sqn, Acklington, August 1940

This aircraft wears Des Sheen's distinctive boomerang badge on its cockpit entry hatch. Whilst flying an earlier production Mk I (K9959) emblazoned with this unique marking, the Australian pilot shot down a He 115 on 21 October 1939 and claimed a third of a kill against a He 111 on 7 December that same year – the fighter (and the pilot) was hit during this latter engagement.

16

Mk I K9953/ZP-A of Flt Lt Adolf Malan, No 74 Sqn, Hornchurch, May/June 1940

Malan was flying this aircraft on 27 May when he claimed a Bf 109E destroyed, two Do 17s damaged and an unconfirmed half kill over a third Dornier bomber near Calais – the final claim was shared with Plt Off P C F Stevenson (2 shared destroyed, 6 unconfirmed destroyed and 5 damaged). He also used K9953 during the remarkable action on the night of 18/19 June, as described in chapter one, when he shot down two He 111s from KG 4. After the Battle of Britain the aircraft went to No 7 OTU, before being passed on to No 57 OTU, where it was wrecked in a collision on 7 October 1943.

17

Mk IIA P8194/DL-M *Gold Coast I* of Sgt Donald McKay, No 91 Sqn, Hawkinge, April 1941

Flying Spitfire Mk Is and IIAs, McKay was credited with 6 enemy aircraft destroyed and three damaged – his total victory score was 14 enemy aircraft destroyed and 4 damaged. This presentation aircraft later served with Nos 234, 66 and 152 Sqns. After a spell with No 57 OTU, this Spitfire was employed in trials in 1943 with a reversible-pitch propeller to shorten the landing run. It was written off in March 1944.

18

Mk I R6596/QJ-S of Plt Off Alan Wright, No 92 Sqn, Pembrey, August 1940

Throughout his operational career, Wright's personal aircraft always carried the identification letter 'S'. He was flying this aircraft on the night of 14/15 August when he shared in the destruction of a He 111P of 9./KG 27 sent to bomb Cardiff docks. Two of the other three pilots also credited with destroying this bomber were aces with No 92 Sqn – Flt Lt R S Tuck and Plt Off D G Williams (5 and 1 shared destroyed, 1 and 1 unconfirmed destroyed, 2 probables and 6 damaged). Wright's final score was 11 and 3 shared destroyed, 2 'possibly destroyed', 5 probables and 7 damaged. Aside from the shared He 111, Wright also used R6596 to down a second Heinkel at night on 29 August and a third during the day on 11 September – he also claimed a Bf 109E probable on this latter date. Late in the afternoon of 9 September 1940 Wright was bounced by Bf 109Es whilst patrolling over Biggin Hill, and he only just managed to land the badly damaged R6596 back at base. Following repairs, it spent a few months with No 131 Sqn during 1941, before going to No 52 OTU in October. It was written off whilst with No 57 OTU in April 1944.

19

Mk I N3249/QJ-P of Sgt Ralph Havercroft, No 92 Sqn, Pembrey, August 1940

Delivered to No 92 Sqn in late December 1939 as one of the first Spitfires issued to the unit as replacements for their Blenheim IFs, this aircraft was damaged during a night landing at Bibury on 31 August, but was repaired and allocated to No 602 Sqn in early November. It was lost whilst serving with this unit in Scotland on 14 February 1941. 'Titch' Havercroft's final score was 3 and 1 shared destroyed, 2 unconfirmed destroyed, 1 and 1 shared probable and 3 damaged.

20

Mk IB R6908/QJ-F of Flt Lt Brian Kingcome, No 92 Sqn, Biggin Hill, November 1940

One of the first Spitfires to go into service fitted with a mixed cannon and machine gun armament, this aircraft was later converted to Mk V standard. After suffering damage in a low-level engagement over the Channel in one of the first actions involving Bf 109Fs (of Stab./JG 53) on 9 May 1941, R6908 was crash-landed back at Biggin Hill by its wounded pilot, Plt Off Maitland-Thompson, and written off. Brian Kingcome's wartime score was 8 and 3 shared destroyed, 1 shared unconfirmed destroyed, 5 probables and 13 damaged.

21

Mk I X4036/D-AZ of Plt Off Robert Doe, No 234 Sqn, Middle Wallop, August 1940

Although flown on numerous occasions during the summer of 1940 by Bob Doe, this machine was also used on the afternoon of 18 August by leading No 234 Sqn ace Flg Off Patterson Hughes to down two Bf 109Es (of 1./JG 27) off the Isle of Wight. Doe also claimed one *Emil* destroyed and one damaged during this action, the German fighters attempting to protect a large formation of Ju 87s sent to knock out the CH radar station at Poling, in West Sussex, and several naval airfields on the south coast. X4036 later served with No 66 Sqn in the spring of 1941, before passing to No 52 OTU.

22

Mk II P8081/DU-R *GARFIELD WESTON IV* of Flt Lt Adolphe Vybiral, No 312 'Czech' Sqn, Ayr, November 1941

Adolphe Vybiral escaped from Czechoslovakia and joined the French Air Force, and during the Battle of France was credited with downing seven aircraft whilst flying Curtiss Hawk 75 fighters. He escaped to England and joined No 312 Sqn, which he later commanded. Prior to being issued to the Czechs, P8081 had seen service with Nos 222 and 452 Sqns.

23

Mk I L1004/LO-Q of Sqn Ldr Alexander 'Sandy' Johnstone, OC No 602 Sqn, Drem, June 1940

Johnstone was flying this aircraft on the night of 25/26 June when he shot down a He 111H-3 of 3./KG 26 near Dunbar. Five days later he was credited with a shared kill (again in L1004) after mortally damaging a I./KG 51 Ju 88, the other pilot involved in the action being Flg Off P Webb (3 and 3 shared destroyed and 5 damaged). On 3 July he used the machine to damage a Do 17 – Johnstone's finally tally was 7 and 2 shared destroyed, 1 probable and 6 and 1 shared damaged. After a year in the frontline, L1004 spent time with No 58 OTU before being modified into a Mk V in mid-1941. Later still it became the second prototype PR Mk XIII, before being re-configured in early 1944 as the Seafire Mk III prototype.

24

Mk I L1019/LO-G of Sgt Basil Whall, No 602 Sqn, Westhampnett, August 1940

Whall was flying this aircraft on the afternoon of 18 August when he shot down two Ju 87B-1s of II. and III./StG 77 that had attacked Ford airfield. Whilst attacking the second Stuka, L1019 took hits to the engine from the dive-bomber's rear gunner and Whall was forced to ditch the aircraft in shallow water off Bognor Regis. Basil Whall died from injuries received whilst attempting to crash land battle damaged X4160 following combat with a Ju 88 off Beachy Head on 7 October 1940 – his score then stood at 7 destroyed and 2 shared destroyed and 1 and 1 shared probably destroyed.

25

Mk I X4382/LO-G of Plt Off Osgood Hanbury, No 602 Sqn, Westhampnett, September 1940

Hanbury used X4382 to destroy of a Bf 110 near Beachy Head on 15 September, half a Ju 88 over Tangmere on 21 September and a second Ju 88 on 30 September near Selsey-Bembridge. His final score was 10 and 2 shared, 2 probables and 3 and 2 damaged. In December 1940 X4382 was passed to No 610 Sqn for a few months before becoming an OTU aircraft – it had one final 'fling' in the frontline, however, serving for several weeks with No 412 'Falcon' Sqn, RCAF, in July/August 1941. It was struck off charge in January 1945.

26

Mk I X4541/LO-M of Sgt Cyril Babbage, No 602 Sqn, Westhampnett, October 1940

Babbage was flying this aircraft on 12 October when he shared in the destruction of a Ju 88A-1 of II./LG 1 with Canadian Flg Off J S Hart off Beachy Head. Both Spitfires were hit by return fire, however, and X4541 ended up on its back in a field in Sussex following Babbage's forced landing – although the fighter was a write off, the pilot was unhurt. Babbage's final wartime tally was 7 and 1 shared destroyed, 2 and 1 shared probables and 2 damaged.

27

Mk I L1067/XT-D of Sqn Ldr George Denholm, OC No 603 Sqn, Aberdeen/Dyce, March 1940

Denholm saw considerable action in this Spitfire between March and August 1940, damaging a Do 17 on 17 March, followed by an unconfirmed kill over a He 111 on 26 June, a third of a kill against another 'He 111' (actually a Ju 88) on 3 July and a Bf 109E probable on 28 August. Two days latter he baled out of L1067 following combat with Bf 110Cs of II./ZG 76 over Deal, but was back in action the following day. Denholm's final score was 3 and 3 shared destroyed, 1 unconfirmed destroyed, 3 and 1 shared probables and 6 damaged.

28

Mk I R6835/XT-W of Flg Off Brian Carbury, No 603 Sqn, Hornchurch, August 1940

Possibly the most successful pilot/aircraft combination in Fighter Command in the summer of 1940, Carbury used R6835 to shoot down eight Bf 109Es between 29 August and 2 September, with five of these kills being scored during three patrols flown on 31 August – he had built up to this 'ace in a day' feat by claiming single *Emils* on the 29th and 30th. During the final combat in the early evening of the 31st, No 603 Sqn tangled with elements of I./JG 3 over the Thames Estuary, and after claiming two Bf 109s Carbury's Spitfire was hit by a 20 mm round which knocked out its compressed air system. Badly damaged by an exploding oxygen bottle, R6835 took ten months to repair, and was finally reissued to No 457 Sqn (RAAF) in June 1941. It then served with various OTUs, before being passed to the Fleet Air Arm in May 1943.

29

Mk I X4277/XT-M of Flg Off Richard Hillary, No 603 Sqn, Hornchurch

Australian Hillary also met with success on 31 August when he used this aircraft to down a Bf 109 over Dungeness – he had inadvertently formed up with a formation of *Emils* thinking they were Hurricanes after becoming separated from his own unit! After downing one fighter, he bade a hasty retreat undetected. Hillary scored three more kills over Emils, and claimed one as a probable and one damaged, in X4277 before being shot down in flames in the fighter off Margate on 3 September by Hauptmann Bode of II./JG 26. Badly burned, Hillary somehow managed to bail out of the stricken fighter and was rescued by the Margate lifeboat. During his many months in hospital recovering from his severe facial burns he wrote *The Last Enemy*, describing his training, experience in combat and subsequent recovery – upon its release in 1942 it became an instant classic on the Battle of Britain period. His victory score was 5 enemy aircraft destroyed, 2 probably destroyed and 1 damaged, all during the Battle. Hillary was killed in a Blenheim crash on 8 January 1943.

30

Mk I N3288/XT-H of Plt Off George Gilroy, No 603 Sqn, Biggin Hill, August 1940

Gilroy was also successfully involved in No 603 Sqn's hectic day of action on 31 August, using this fighter to claim a Bf 109 destroyed – the combination had earlier downed an *Emil* over Kent two days previously. Gilroy's score by war's end stood at 14 and 10 shared destroyed, 2 shared probables, 5 and 4 shared damaged and 3 shared destroyed on the ground. N3288 went on to serve with Nos 609, 65, 145 and

123 Sqns, before being retired to No 58 OTU in November 1941. In February 1943 it became an instructional airframe, and was finally struck off charge in May 1945.

31
Mk I X4250/XT-X of Sgt Jack Stokoe, No 603 Sqn, Biggin Hill, August 1940

Stokoe also claimed a Bf 109 on the evening patrol over the Thames Estuary on 31 August when he used X4250 to down E-4 Werk-Nr 1503 of 3./JG 3, flown by Oberleutnant W Binder – he was credited with a second *Emil* as having been probably destroyed. This Spitfire was written off in a forced landing on Folkstone beach on 27 September by South African Plt Off P G Dexter (5 destroyed and 2 probables), who had put the perfectly serviceable fighter down in order to attempt to save his squadron-mate, Plt Off 'Pip' Cardell. The latter had baled out of his battle-damaged Spitfire just offshore, but his parachute had failed to open and he fell to his death.

32
Mk I P9322/PR-L of Plt Off David Crook, No 609 Sqn, Middle Wallop, July 1940

Crook was flying this aircraft on the evening of 9 July when he shot down a Ju 87B of I./StG 77 and damaged a second off Portland naval base – his first aerial victories. He was also credited with a shared damage claim against a Do 17 whilst flying the fighter on 13 July. Crook's final score was 5 and 2 shared destroyed, 2 probables and 1 and 1 shared damaged. Shot up by a Bf 110 of V./LG 1 whilst being flown by Plt Off M J Appleby on 8 August off the Isle of Wight, P9322 underwent extensive repairs before being issued to No 61 OTU. The veteran fighter was written off on 15 September 1942 when it broke up in flight near Cardiff.

33
Mk I R6690/PR-Q of Flg Off John Dundas, No 609 Sqn, Middle Wallop, August 1940

No 609 Sqn's leading ace, John Dundas used this machine on the afternoon of 13 August to down one Ju 87R and damage a second (both from II./StG 2) over Lyme Bay, although the gunner in the latter Stuka managed to knock out R6690's glycol system – Dundas was forced to perform a deadstick landing back at Warmwell. Following a short spell out of action, the Mk I was declared serviceable again later in the month, but was shot down from a height of 20,000 ft just after midday on 15 September whilst attacking a formation of Do 17s over Kenley. Its pilot, Plt Off G N Gaunt, died in the crash.

34
Mk I R6691/PR-J of Flt Lt Frank Howell, No 609 Sqn, Middle Wallop, August 1940

This particular Mk I was heavily involved in combat with No 609 Sqn during the summer of 1940, being used by Frank Howell (7 and 3 shared destroyed, 2 unconfirmed destroyed, 2 probables, 2 and 1 shared damaged) to destroy a Stuka in the same action that involved R6690. The Howell/R6691 combination also destroyed a Bf 110 on 25 August and a Do 17 on 15 September, as well as probable kills on 7 September – some confusion exists over the claim for 25 August , as Sgt Alan Feary (5 destroyed, 1 shared unconfirmed destroyed, 1 probable and 4 damaged) has also been credited with a Bf 110C-4 (of 1./ZG 2) kill, plus one damaged, in R6691 at the same time! On 25 September, whilst being flown by Flg Off J C Newbery, the aircraft was power dived in order to evade Bf 109s, and in the subsequent recovery suffered distorted wings and a shattered hood. In the cockpit, the pilot's seat collapsed due to the G inflicted on the airframe, and Newbery suffered severe internal injuries. Following repairs, R6691 went on to serve with Nos 616 and 602 Sqns, before being passed to No 58 OTU in June 1941. It was finally written off following a mid-air collision with a another OTU Spitfire Mk V in March 1943.

35
Mk IIA P8098/PR-Z *ENFIELD SPITFIRE* of Flt Lt John Curchin, No 609 Sqn, Biggin Hill, May 1941

Although this presentation aircraft was the personal mount of Australian Battle of Britain ace John Curchin (8 and 4 shared destroyed, 1 shared unconfirmed destroyed, 1 probable and 1 damaged), he was actually flying P8264 (see below) when he claimed his only kills (1.5 Bf 109F-2s of I./JG 3) in a Mk IIA on 8 May 1941 – P8098 *had* been involved in this sortie, but was being flown by a Sgt R Boyd. Severely damaged in a forced landing near Manston following combat on 21 May, P8098 underwent extensive repairs before finally being issued to No 130 Sqn in August. Its flying days were ended whilst still in frontline service with the latter unit when it struck a hut during a low altitude beat up of Peranporth airfield in October 1941.

36
Mk IIA P8264/PR-H of Flg Off John Bisdee, No 609 Sqn, Biggin Hill, May 1941

Decorated with the family *fleur de lys* beneath the cockpit, this aircraft was used by John 'The Bishop' Bisdee (8 and 2 shared destroyed, 4 probables and 3 and 1 shared damaged) to claim a half share against a Bf 109 during Circus 10, flown on 21 May. On this day No 609 Sqn, as part of the Biggin Hill Wing, filled the role of Withdrawal Cover for a formation of Blenheims that had bombed an oil refinery at Bethune. As noted above, John Curchin also met with success whilst flying P8264, although the fighter was damaged by enemy fire in this action. The machine later served with Nos 452 and 131 Sqns, then with OTUs and other second line units, including the Empire Central Flying School, until it was struck off charge in December 1944.

37
Mk I R6806/DW-N of Flt Lt John Ellis, No 610 Sqn, Biggin Hill, July 1940

No 610 Sqn's most successful pilot of 1940, John Ellis (13 and 1 shared destroyed, 1 shared unconfirmed destroyed, 1 probable and 2 damaged) achieved ace status in this aircraft on 25 July when, during two successive sorties, he claimed the destruction of three Bf 109Es of III./JG 52 off the Dover coast – the German fighters had been flying as escorts for Do 17s sent to bomb coastal convoys. A highly experienced prewar pilot, Ellis assumed command of No 610 Sqn following the death in action of the previous incumbent, Sqn Ldr A T Smith, on the very same day the former had achieved 'acedom'. R6806 saw much action in the early stages of the Battle, being damaged in combat with Bf 109s on 12 August, and then 'written off' in combat on 2 September whilst being flown by No 72 Sqn OC, Sqn Ldr A R Collins – a number of No 610 Sqn's Spitfires (still wearing DW codes) were left behind at Biggin Hill for the newly arrived No 72 Sqn to use following the former unit's posting 'up north' to No 13 Group for a rest. Collins had been shot up in X4105 earlier that day, and somehow managed to coax R6806 back to Croydon, where it was initially considered to be fit only for scrapping. However, after spending nine months on the ground being repaired, it was test flown and issued to No 132 Sqn in July 1941, before being passed to No 52 OTU the following month. It was struck off charge in March 1945.

38

Mk I P9433/DW-E of Plt Off Constantine Pegge, No 610 Sqn, Biggin Hill, August 1940

Pegge (8 destroyed, 1 probable and 3 damaged) used this aircraft on 12 August to shoot down two Bf 109Es in the Hawkinge/Dover area, his OC, John Ellis, also accounting for an *Emil* confirmed and a second as a probable during the course of this sortie. Twelve days later the Pegge/P9433 combination claimed another Bf 109E as a probable north of Gravesend. This aircraft had earlier served with No 92 Sqn, and following the Battle of Britain was overhauled, before being operated by No 131 Sqn in September 1941. Soon replaced by a Mk V, R9433 saw out its remaining years with a succession of OTUs and other second line units, before finally being struck off charge in October 1944.

39

Mk I X4253/N-FY of Sgt Wilfred Duncan-Smith, No 611 Sqn, Rochford, December 1940

Destined to go on and score 17 kills (and numerous probables and damaged claims) in various marks of Spitfire in a long and distinguished career in the frontline, Wilfred Duncan-Smith saw his first action in this Mk I on 29 December when he was credited with a half share in the probable destruction of a Do 17Z from II./KG 3 near Burnham on Crouch. A Battle of Britain veteran that had served with Nos 266 and 41 Sqns, X4253 was later used as a training tool by a series of second line units.

40

Mk IIA P7531/L-Z-I of Flt Lt Charles Green, No 421 Flt, Hawkinge, November 1940

Charles Green (11 destroyed, 3 and 1 shared probable and 1 damaged) commanded this unique flight, which was assigned the task of tracking incoming enemy formations and reporting on their composition and altitude. It inherited the 'LZ' code letters of No 66 Sqn, from which it formed, but with a square dot separating the two letters. Green was credited with 1 enemy aircraft destroyed and 2 probably destroyed whilst serving with No 421 Flt, although the identity of the Spitfire used to score these kills remains unrecorded. Prior to being issued to the Flight P7531 had been employed in diving trials at RAE Farnborough, and went on to serve with No 91 Sqn when No 421 Flt was expanded into a full squadron in January 1941. The Spitfire was subsequently shot down by I./JG 2's Unteroffizier Amhausend off Ostend whilst on a low-level shipping reconnaissance sortie on the afternoon of 24 April, its pilot, Plt Off Peall, baling out safely.

FIGURE PLATES

1

Plt Off David M Crook of No 609 Sqn at Middle Wallop in early September 1940. The weather in the south-west was particularly warm late into the summer of 1940, and many No 10 Group pilots favoured a combination of Battle Dress trousers and a bright pale blue (faded to almost white) shirt and black tie. Crook has also chosen to wear steel-tipped shoes as opposed to the more typical 1936 Pattern flying boots. His life jacket is a 1932 Pattern issue, with yellow-painted front panels to heighten visibility for Air Sea Rescue units searching for downed pilots in the Channel.

2

Flt Sgt George C Unwin and 'Flash', both of No 19 Sqn at Duxford in June 1940. The former is wearing full Battle Dress (note the eagle badge of the NCO airman on his right sleeve), complemented with a white scarf around his neck to reduce chafing whilst keeping a 'look out' for the enemy. Like the other figures on this plate, Unwin is wearing a Type B helmet, fitted with a Type D (Type 19) oxygen mask, and a 1932 Pattern life jacket, although he has refrained from adding yellow panels to the latter at this early stage in the conflict. Finally, his flying boots are 1936 Pattern issue.

3

One of 24 Fleet Air Arm pilots temporarily transferred to the RAF in mid-1940, Sub-Lt Arthur G 'Admiral' Blake served with No 19 Sqn from July to 29 October, when he was shot down and killed. He is wearing standard Royal Navy Officer's Dress, complemented with a white neck scarf. Note the 'A' for 'Air' within the rank curl on Blake's left sleeve, as well as the naval pilot's brevet. Like Unwin and Crook, his life jacket is a 1932 Pattern issue, coloured yellow at squadron level.

4

Sqn Ldr John A Kent (12 destroyed, 3 probables and 2 damaged), OC of No 92 Sqn at Biggin Hill in November 1940. With the winter weather closing in, many pilots now took to wearing the jackets of their 1938 Pattern Irvin flying suits whilst aloft. Kent's Type B helmet has been modified to allow him to wear the Mk IV goggles depicted here – these had only been issued in mid-1940. His gloves appear to have been privately acquired, but his boots are standard 1936 Pattern.

5

Top button of his Battle Dress undone in true fighter pilot's fashion, Plt Off Desmond G Williams of No 92 Sqn is seen in May 1940 at Northolt. Devoid of a life jacket, the pilot's harness arrangement for his seat-type parachute is clearly visible. Williams' boots are 1936 Pattern whilst his gloves are of unknown origin. He was lost on 10 October 1940 when he collided with 8-kill ace Flg Off J F Drummond (also of No 92 Sqn) whilst attacking a Do 17 – the latter was also killed.

6

Sqn Ldr Donald O Finlay, OC No 41 Sqn at Hornchurch in November 1940, wears a relatively rare pre-war lightweight one-piece overall (made of cotton twill), standard 1932 Pattern life jacket, polo neck sweater and 1936 Pattern flying boots.